FROM LAWYER TO MISSIONARY:
A JOURNEY TO KENYA AND BACK AGAIN

CARRIE REICHARTZ

THIS BOOK IS DEDICATED TO

My aunt Karen Christian who started me on this
adoption journey so long ago.
My Kenyan teammates Allan and Eve Owano without
whom none of my Kenyan work would be possible.
My friend, mentor, and so much more, Pat Molitor, who
came alongside me years ago and, at the times when I wanted
to give up, she gave me encouragement and courage to continue.
I could, and would not have done this without her.

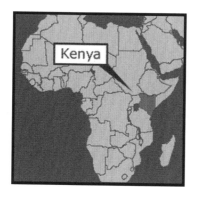

Published in 2012

www.fromlawyertomissionary.com
www.kenyagivehope.com

Copyright © in published edition Carrie Reichartz

ISBN 978-0-9859456-0-2

CONTENTS

4

5

6

7

Getting There is Half the Battle, I Hope · 125

8

Remember Me · 153

9

Ways of Making a Difference · 171

ACKNOWLEDGEMENTS

Penny Swift. Patience, motivation, endless edits, and willing to come alongside me for a great cause with great advice and guidance. Thank you so much, Penny. You did much more work than what you were paid to do and it is not overlooked. I could not have done this without you.

Chris Reichartz, my husband, for his patience and helping me with time for writing and keeping me focused and 'doing everything' while I was writing, and always!

My parents: Connie Randlett, my mom, for her example. Read more in the book. Roger and Susie Weber, my dad and second mom, for being wonderful parents and teaching me so much about life and myself, especially money, and for their formatting advice and encouragement.

My kids: Colton Watkins, my son, for his servant heart to help others with his quiet personality. Brooklyn Watkins, my daughter, for extensive help and feedback with the photos and other parts of the book, as well as being an inspiration with her servant's heart.

My friends: Michelle Jacobson, my best friend forever, for her expert formatting advice from her endless reading of books over the years. Pat Molitor for her amazing photos that you will see throughout this book and on the cover, and for her endless feedback, advice, and editing. Paul Odhiambo, friend, for the stories, pictures, and continuing the mission. Emilly Akoth, friend, for the stories and continuing the mission. Kristen Pettigrew, friend, for being a partner and inspiration in the Kenyan work.

My leaders and Guides: Jim and Susie Horne, missionaries to Mombasa, Kenya for over 30 years, for their amazing dedication to the Kenyan kids and people which rubs off on everyone they come into contact with. And for their guidance and direction through all of this process. Bobby and Lisa Bechtel, missionaries to Mombasa, Kenya for their amazing work and life lived for God and adoption. Guy and Denise Conn who taught me and continue teaching me to believe in a HUGE God and not myself. Thank you guys.

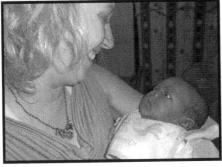

Above: A young orphan carries her sibling on her back in a village in Kenya.

Left: Carrie with an abandoned baby in Kenya.

7

INTRODUCTION

What do you envision when you think of Africa? The Dark Continent! Jungles, spreading acacia trees, and haunting landscapes? Tremendous beauty savannahs filled with animals hunting for food? Masai warriors, tall and dressed in red, their spears glistening in a burning sunset? Surging waves of the stark blue Indian Ocean? Do you also see agonizing despair, poverty, hunger, AIDS, and civil war? How can a place own so much beauty and chaos at the same time?

Traveling to the eastern edge of Kenya, at the start of the southern part of Africa, just under the horn, you will find Kenya... a country divided by the equator. There is a tremendous difference in temperature between the interior and the coast, with its humidity. The only port city on the eastern coast of Africa is Mombasa in Kenya. It is sometimes called the Gateway to the East. Its landscape is beautiful... ocean, beaches, all-inclusive resorts that dot the area. But just up the coast you will find quite a different life.

Small child alone on the side of the road.

Kenyans are wonderfully kind, open, friendly, and willing to help wherever needed. They are quick to offer a serving of their native dish, Ugali, which is made from maize flour (cornmeal) and cooked with water to the consistency of dough-like porridge. (It looks like mashed potatoes.) It's the most common staple starch in Kenya. They will happily serve this meal to the strains of African, drum-intensive music and enchanting songs in Swahili. The children are shy, yet friendly. Some are nervous when they encounter different skin color because of their chequered history.

The land and its people are all that I've described. Kenyans are beautiful human beings but their poverty is horrendous. I learned this firsthand. Come along with me as I share my African adventure with you. Perhaps you'll meet some new friends along the way.

Slums are common place.

1

JULY 2008

YOU WANT ME TO GO WHERE?

My first trip to Kenya was in July 2008. It was an amazing journey. However, there is a story before the story, as there usually is.

In November 2006, my friend Monica, who lives four hours north, was in town for the weekend. She had been here the weekend before and had been looking for a specific church that she couldn't find. In her travels, she passed a church and felt drawn in. She really liked it. The next week, when she was staying at my house, she really, really, really wanted to go back. I didn't. I was tired. We had been at Barnes and Noble until after midnight the night before and we had been up talking late; thus, I didn't want to go. Also, I was not a church person. Repeat, *I was not a church person.*

I had grown up in the church, going to both church and Sunday school every week and confirmation classes once a week for a few years. After confirmation, I was done with church. All I felt I heard at church was that I wasn't good enough and that God hated me and everyone else. On the day of my death, He would weigh all of my good things against all of my bad things and, if good outweighed the bad, I would make it to heaven. If not, that other place would be my permanent home. I also had my share of run-ins with 'churchie' type people. You know the ones. They never seemed happy; they always had rules; they were usually not friendly. However, they loved their church and thought you needed to be there. They talked good church talk, but their lives were something totally different. I wanted no part of that. I just wanted to be a good person and have that be enough. In reality, I was not interested in church.

I believed there was a God of some sort; I just didn't have any idea how this whole thing called life worked. Looking at nature and how everything ran so smoothly, there had to be something out there holding things together, but I didn't have any idea what or who.

The extent of my spirituality was going to Al-Anon to try to deal with drinking issues in my life, and taking a course through the Center for Creative Learning, *Taking It Lightly*, that left me feeling free and great. At that point, I felt that, if I just read enough, and read the right books, and did the right things, I could keep this great peaceful feeling. But if I didn't get the right books, or see the right Oprah show, or do the right things, then things seemed to fall apart really quickly. It was a stressful spirituality and it all came down to me, my work, and becoming perfect. If I didn't do it exactly the right way, things would blow up on me. This brought some peace, but also a lot of stress and expectations.

When Monica asked me to go to this church she had found, I really didn't want to go because I didn't want to hear yet again how bad I was and how angry God was with me; nor did I want to run into those 'churchie' types. Why waste a perfectly good Sunday at church? Monica insisted, so I finally just said, "Fine, it's only an hour". We headed off to this church my friend loved… Fox River Christian Church in Waukesha, Wisconsin. We couldn't find it right away, so we arrived late.

This church seemed different from all the ones I had been familiar with. For instance, there was a rock band playing some really good music. I never imagined church to be like this. People were friendly and not 'fake' church friendly either. The message was excellent and down to earth. The pastor didn't try to act like he had everything all figured out. He didn't say that, if we would just listen and do what he said, we'd be perfect. Rather, he spoke about how our lives are **not** perfect; that it isn't always easy; that there's not some other ideal world out there.

I could feel and hear something different in this place, something far different to the churches and the 'churchie' people I had grown up with. Their motto was, "Come as you are" – sweats, bowling shirts, whatever, just come. That's all; nothing more. They didn't ask for money; no crazy 'church' talk.

It's not about appearance; rather, it's about one's heart and moving forward together with God. At the time, I had no idea what that meant, but it sounded a lot better than waiting till the day I died and letting God decide if I was good enough or working hard to be perfect.

After the service, they gave us Starbuck's gift cards and, later that day, representatives of the church stopped by with chocolate chip cookies. They were there, not to have a ten-minute weirdo conversation about what I needed to do to save myself or some other craziness, but just to drop off a package of cookies and said "thanks for coming". They left within less than a few minutes. I was so impressed I kept going back.

In December 2006, Fox River did a *My Gift for Jesus* campaign. The idea behind this request is that we give hundreds or even thousands of dollars in gifts to our family and friends during the Christmas season, but what are we giving to the Birthday Boy? Think about what that meant and decide what we could give to Jesus for His birthday. All the money raised was to go towards mission work, specifically, to the two schools and feeding centers in Kenya that Fox River supports.

In the church, they had videos up on the screen, showing the Kenyan kids singing and saying "thank you" and "Merry Christmas". When I saw the video and heard the powerful background music, it brought tears to my eyes. In all honesty, they weren't just tears, rather bawling week after week as they played the same video over and over. Given this strong reaction, I felt led to apply for the mission trip to Kenya that Fox River offered in July 2007; but I pulled back. I didn't know ANYONE at this church. I had only started attending a month before. Apart from which, as I have said, I am not a church person.

I thought that, at some point, this church would prove to be just like the rest and I would move on. Besides, I had never had a desire to go to any foreign country, least of all Africa. It's far away, the trip is long, and it's expensive. In addition, a few years earlier I had a blood clot in my leg and my lung, and long airplane travel was something I was instructed to avoid, given that life-threatening condition. So in 2007 I said no, giving lots of justification for not signing up.

As 2007 progressed and I continued to enjoy the teachings at Fox River, the rug was suddenly slipped out from under me. I was divorced and had two children, a boy, Colton, then 12 and a girl, Brooklyn, who was 10.

One evening in late April, their dad's sister called to tell me that their father had just passed away unexpectedly. I felt like I was freefalling. Luckily, my kids were out of town so I had a few days to get my feet back on the ground before having to talk with them. My good friend, Michelle, helped me find the words to break the news to the kids. Thank God I was at Fox River because nothing in my previous spiritual experiences could ever have pulled me through that time. I was anxiety-ridden as to how to support and help my kids. I didn't know what it was like to not have a father, so I couldn't relate, and didn't know what they needed. I was shattered. How could they deal with this and why should they have to?

Fox River was very supportive during this time.

By October, I felt God pulling at my heart to join a

Bible study group. The idea seemed crazy. Others in Bible study groups had been studying the Bible for years. I would look like an idiot. I thought that those people had the Bible memorized and could recite verses with ease, whereas I didn't even know how to open the book and find a verse. But the thought of attending a study group kept coming up again and again.

Finally, I went online just to look at a few studies at Elmbrook Church and at Fox River. A few weeks later, I began studying at Fox River. We read a book about *Being Mary In a Martha World*. Of course at first I thought the book was about Martha Stewart, but as it turned out, there was a story in the Bible about two sisters – Mary and Martha. Martha was just like Martha Stewart and her sister Mary was a bit more relaxed. The group I studied with consisted mostly of people new to Bible study. This was the beginning of making some connections, not only at Fox River but also in my life, which finally started to have a greater purpose and was starting to be less about me.

I had always been searching for something to make life make sense, or have purpose, but I could never figure out what that was. Now everything was beginning to make more sense. I didn't have to read all the self-help books or discover the 'new thing' and have all the knowledge. I could see and feel that something was changing. It wasn't all up to me alone to figure it out. I still didn't understand it, but I could see evidence of it in my life.

In December, the *My Gift for Jesus* video presentations came up again. This year the song was, *Do They Know It's Christmas Time At All*. This song was one I had always loved. Every week, for the next five or six weeks, I cried hysterically, unable to stop. "Why do I get to live here like I want, and they are there and don't even know it is Christmas, or what Christmas even means?" How can I ignore them and their problems and pretend they don't exist?

When the meeting for the 2008 trip to Kenya was announced, I said, "OK, God, I will go to the meeting, but I'm not making any commitments." I decided to get more information, but I still had no desire to go to Kenya. Besides, I didn't know anyone else who was going. At the meeting, I met people who had gone the previous year. Story after story was told about life change, marriage, money miracles, and so much more. From the end of December 2007 through February 2008 there had been troubles with the presidential election that led to riots and killings, and a lot of trouble for Kenya. With this backdrop, I had to make a decision. I had no idea why or how, but I KNEW, I **had** to go.

While at the meeting one woman, Rosie, had shared how she brought her nine-year-old son with her on the trip. That got some wheels going in my head. Colton's dad had passed away a few months earlier. I was doing the best I could, but I had a nagging feeling that he felt different to other kids because everyone else had a mom and a dad and he didn't, which could lead to self-pity. I felt compelled to take my 13-year-old son, Colton, along with me so he could see that he might have a different life than some kids here, but that he had a great life compared with kids in other parts of the world.

Colton is a lot like his dad; how can I say, stubborn. You could ask the boy if he wanted a million dollars and his immediate answer would be "no". That is just how he is. I came home from the meeting and immediately went upstairs to his room to ask him if he would be interested. Before I even asked, I told him not to answer me that night. I told him to think about it and let me know. I told him a bit about the opportunity, and he immediately answered "yes".

The decision to go was made, but now the question remained as to how we were going to finance this venture. I'm a single mom doing the best I can to support two kids by running my own small law practice. We are living all right financially, but having to add US$7,000 in expenses for the trip in just a few months was not going to happen. I prayed and prayed and had other people pray. This was a new thing for me. I had no experience with prayer or how to listen for answers. I knew the prayers we had to memorize for confirmation, which meant nothing to me whatsoever. But luckily, there were some people around me who knew how to pray, and their prayers seemed to have great results. So I thought I would try it.

After a few weeks, I awoke one night at 3 am and heard in my head, "Send letters to lawyers." That was a bit disturbing. I had never had that experience and didn't know how to label it.

The next day I started drafting a letter outlining what we wanted to do for the Kenyan kids, and why I wanted Colton to come on this trip. It was difficult for me to write the letter, especially sending it out to the legal community, because I don't like to publicize my personal life. I like to keep it professional, but I didn't have any other financial options. It took many hours of work to write that letter, getting it just 'perfect'; reading every name in the Wisconsin Lawyer (a phone book of lawyers that is about 300 pages long); and sending it to anyone whose name I recognized, even if I didn't remember from where; typing addresses, stuffing envelopes, folding letters, return envelopes, etcetera. Colton and Brooklyn helped with the stuffing and labeling. I prayed and prayed… and waited.

I was amazed by the response. It was neat to see who did or did not send money. Some people that I totally didn't expect (based on personalities and working with them), did send funds. Some people that I hardly knew sent funds, too. There were also some whom I thought would surely support, who did not. God had it all worked out.

Now I can look back and realize that it was God's voice that woke me up that night with those words. This was confirmed after I also sent the letter to some other places that God did not direct me to. The amount of money I spent on stamps and so on did not even come close to covering what came in on those non-God directed letters.

We received about US$11 from those efforts and had spent over US$100 to send them out, whereas the lawyer letters brought in about US$6,500, almost enough for both of our trips. The prayer had definitely worked. I cannot explain it, but it worked.

All that withstanding, there was still financial struggle. I had recently started my own law practice, and hadn't even completed the first year of the business, which is not usually the most profitable time for a business. Businesses, especially new ones, have ebbs and flow of income. Spring 2008 was definitely an ebb period. I didn't even have enough money coming in to cover our house payment and bills.

There was a moment or two when I seriously considered canceling the trip due to money constraints. One day prior to us leaving, God provided the entire amount we needed through a general donation to the church. What a miraculous answer to prayer! However, greater miracles and changes were in store for us once we arrived in Kenya.

From January through June 2008 we had met at Fox River once a month to learn about Kenya and its culture. We worked out the plan of our trip and got to know the group a little better. Our principle reason for going was to spend time with the kids in the schools that Fox River fully supports.

At these meetings we brainstormed, as a group, how to accomplish this. What sorts of things did we need to take with us? After much animated discussion, we decided on several activities, specifically a craft, jump ropes, and a Bible lesson for the kids. Colton suggested bringing basketball to the kids. The group agreed. The church had the hoops installed before we got there and we took deflated balls with us in the suitcases.

After months of preparation and financing, it was finally time to go. Once in Kenya, I was unprepared for the devastating poverty we would encounter.

People live in mud huts with no running water, not even any clean water... Kids walk three miles or more for dirty water. Three- and four-year-olds, carry infants on their backs all day. Kids from the villages followed us around during the day, on a school day. While they were obviously old enough to be in school, they could not afford the school fees, and so stayed at home.

Kids and their parents are starving – they didn't even have one meal a day. This is what I had seen in my third-grade social studies book, but, I thought no-one really lived like this anymore. Those were pictures from a long time ago, not now. But here, almost 30 years after looking at those images in my textbook, people were still living like that every day. I had no idea. It was hard to think about people living like this while I'm at home going into debt for jewelry, a nice car, clothes, or whatever else my heart desires.

We had two days of 'community outreach', where the community was invited to come to the school for a soccer tournament, choir competition, and a free meal. You saw very few smiles, happiness, or joy. Thousands of people, who had come from the villages around the area, were served a bowl of rice and some beans that day. For many, this was the best and largest meal they would have all year. I saw little hope. They were very, very quiet and afraid of us.

There have been years of racial problems in Kenya, and that has left local people afraid of people with white skin. Little children would run away from us screaming as we walked through the villages. They didn't understand English well, especially with our 'accent'. (English-speaking Kenyans speak with a British accent as the country is a former British colony.) Somehow, though, we managed to communicate that we loved them.

Other than the schools our church supports, and the small minority of kids (about 200 at this time) who get to attend for free and get fed every school day, there was very little hope. The only spark of hope we saw were the kids at the schools. In the villages, the kids' eyes appeared dark and bleak and their clothes were tattered at best. This broke my heart.

This reality was illustrated by something as simple as a pen. During one of the community outreach events, I had been wandering around, and a few kids came up and grabbed my hand and were walking around with me. I looked in my small travel purse to see what we could do together. I had a pen and some gum wrappers. They saw the pen and communicated, without words, that they would like to use it. I told them I didn't have any paper. They saw the gum wrappers and asked to use those. (Everything is recycled or repurposed in Kenya, even gum wrappers. They don't even have garbage cans.) So they wrote their numbers and their letters and a few other things. They were so grateful just to have a chance to use a pen for a few minutes and to be able to practice writing. It was as though they were given the newest video game system at the time, PlayStation III. But it was simply a pen.

We, as Americans, have many pens lying around our houses and never think anything about them. A simple pen was more than Christmas to these kids, and they were only using it temporarily. That was one of many coming moments, when my heart and eyes were opened to see how blessed we are in America and we don't even know it.

One of the girls I met that day had to be about ten years old. She had her baby brother on her back the whole day. I encouraged her to write with us, but she refused again and again. She would not set the baby down off her back. After an hour or more, she finally did let me hold the baby for her, but she continued to just watch the other kids write. I finally pushed a pen into her hand and placed a small piece of paper in front of her, but she didn't know how to write. She merely scribbled, like when a child is little and tries to copy their parents' cursive writing, but can only scribble and scribble. That's what this child did. She was ten and couldn't even write numbers or letters, instead, she walked around with a baby on her back.

That is the reality of life in Kenya for most kids and it devastates me. We take school for granted and complain about going. This girl doesn't have that luxury and never will. She would no doubt continue to care for her younger siblings and then, hopefully, would get married to someone with a job and take care of her own kids, who more than likely would repeat the same pattern. Could this be real in 2008?

It brings tears to my eyes to write this but unfortunately, for her, and many more like her, it is their reality and it will not change in her lifetime. Hopefully, it will for her children, but it won't if we don't step up.

REMEMBER ME

Colton is a really quiet kid. He keeps things to himself and it is usually somewhat of a miracle to get him to talk more than a few words at a time. At the end of the community day, where Colton spent all day playing basketball with some 20 year-old Kenyan guys, one of them ran up to him as he was about to leave for the bus and said, "Remember us." Colton then got on the bus to head back to the hotel. He related this story to me right away after he boarded the bus, which, again for a teenage boy, and Colton specifically, was nothing short of miraculous. Those words really touched him.

"Remember us." We hear that all the time from Kenyans. They feel like a forgotten people. All they want is to be remembered.

They feel forgotten by their own people, their government, and the world. I remembered this as I put together my scrapbook commemorating the trip for 2008. I took the time to 'remember' each person. In fact, I could not throw anyone out. I cut around and cut around the pictures in order to include every person that hit my camera in my scrapbook. I had over 1,000 photos and most of them had five or more people in them. This would not have happened if it wasn't for the help of my best friend Michelle Jacobson, who probably cut around more people than I did, as I was assembling them in collage form in the book.

On a very small scale, many, many Kenyans are forever memorialized in those pictures and those albums that I often look at and share with others.

A year later, a good friend of mine, Donna Walbert, took one of the scrapbooks and surprised me with a huge, laminated poster of all the scrapbook pages from that year. My eternal thanks goes to her for this beautiful tribute. This poster was taken to Kenya and is now posted on a wall in the Bible college there for all Kenyans to realize that they are not forgotten.

On a larger scale, I'm hoping that writing, speaking, and sharing their stories will help others become aware, and that they may 'remember them' as they go about their business at the store purchasing things or at home spending their free time surfing the Internet, or watching TV mindlessly when they could be doing one small something to make a difference in the world. It could be something as small as collecting change or cans and donating the proceeds to a cause that God puts on their hearts or writing a note to someone and encouraging them.

LEAVING IS HARD
AND ADJUSTING BACK HOME IS HARDER

After a ten-day visit, I was quite upset as I left, crying well before we got to the airport. At the airport I cried even harder, realizing I had to leave, and not knowing why or what, if anything, I was to do with Kenya or anywhere and also not knowing if I would ever return.

Our group on this trip had really bonded. The 2008 Kenya group continued getting together regularly after we got back. In those get-togethers, we socialized as well as developed committees to work on various projects so we could somehow make a difference.

We constructed a website for the Kenya mission for the church, placed a demonstration table in the gym every week that the people could visit and learn about upcoming trips and watch a video of the last trip, and worked on a DVD project to raise more funds for works in Kenya. It was a great experience. We had a new 'Kenyan family' that met quarterly for dinner and sharing.

The trip had changed me, but I didn't know what to do about the changes, or even what it all meant. I knew I could never again be the person I was before the trip, but didn't know how to be any other way.

My heart and soul had been left in Kenya and I hoped so much to return. I felt like I should do more for the people in Kenya, but I didn't yet know what it was. There were a lot of tears and a lot of confusion, but ever so slowly plans came together.

It took over a month to recover physically with the changed sleep schedule and eating. I had a few hospital visits upon returning, and was extremely anxious about the thought that the blood clot was acting up in my leg. The scans of my left leg showed it filled with clot; and it will continue to look like this permanently from the previous situation. The doctors will never be able to tell if the clot is returning until after it travels somewhere outside of my leg, lungs or brain. It turned out to be a false alarm.

I never fully recovered spiritually or emotionally from this trip, but that's not a bad thing. I was devastated and embarrassed about how I had lived up to this point. I was ashamed at how I had ignored this reality by focusing only on me and my wants. Even simple things like going to Wal-Mart or the grocery store had become incredibly difficult. Seeing all the surplus and knowing that the Kenyans and others had NOTHING. I held a rummage sale and sold a lot of my stuff. I even wanted to sell my house and move to Kenya immediately to help but that was not what was in store for me yet.

MONEY WILL NEVER BE THE SAME

After going financially crazy in college, I have always been fairly conservative with money, or so I thought. I didn't go too overboard, by American standards. However, after Kenya, I began to donate more and more to causes of all types, but especially Africa. I began to see every purchase though the lens of whether or not any item is really worth the money it costs to buy it. I'd tell myself, "Remember, Carrie, it costs only US$20 a month to educate, clothe, and feed children twice a day for a month. Is this (shirt, CD, dinner out) worth it?" I couldn't buy like I used to. It wasn't a sacrifice, it was a choice, and one I could make easily after seeing what I had seen. What is more important, me and my WANTS, or those kids and their minimal NEEDS? My attitude toward money was very much changing.

FROM LAWYER TO WHAT?

There were also changes in store for my career.

While in Kenya, I remembered one of my biggest dreams as a child and all the way through my senior year in high school – to work at a day care facility. As a kid, all my play involved nursery school and day care. My room was laid out like a day care center for all my dolls. I baby-sat and cared for babies whenever I had the chance. But somehow, through a series of events, I ended up in college at UW-Whitewater and then Marquette University at law school. In the hustle and bustle of kids of my own, and life in general, and focusing on making money for that life and those kids… suddenly, here I was in a different space.

I still loved kids and spending time with them, but God had renewed my love to care for kids in another way, in one moment in Kenya. I remember the exact moment. It was during July 2008 while sitting on the ground in Bomani, playing with the baby class (my assignment for the morning). I was sitting with lots of kids – one holding each of my fingers; five kids literally sitting on my lap and about seven more playing with my long blond hair, which to them was just crazy-looking. (There are no blonds in Kenya. Also, most people don't have much hair. Both girls and boys cut it off because they don't have access to water to clean it and it can lead to other health concerns.) As I sat there, I thought to myself, "Why would I not want to do this for the rest of my life? Sitting with kids and having fun and teaching them at the same time…" What a great joy that would be! What a relaxing life! It sure beats presenting people's financial and emotional future into the hands of a judge as a lawyer.

Though at the time I wouldn't have labeled it like this, looking back I would say my first major step with God in my life, other than going to Kenya, was to close my law office. I had worked as a family law lawyer since I got out of law school and, up until the

24

last year before going to Kenya, I loved my work. But over the last year, getting closer and closer to God, I realized He was changing my passion to something else; I just didn't know what that was. Maybe the announcement on Joyce Meyer's TV show, a show I rarely watched at the time, saying, "If God is calling you to open a day care in your home, just do that", should have been a hint back in April of 2008, but it wasn't for me.

After that moment in Kenya, it was clear.

So one month after I returned, I closed most of my private law office practice and opened Almost Home Child Care. The rest, as they say, is history. I'm still doing that and loving every day of working with the kids and teaching them. I took the little more expensive route of US$170,000 in school loans and a trip to Kenya, but God got me back on track!

It was scary. I was going from getting paid US$175 per hour to getting paid US$175 per week for 50 hours of work and hoping I would get enough business in my new venture to earn even that amount. But I had a strange peace about the whole thing.

God has worked in mysterious ways to bring children and parents to the day care center and I am so amazed at His work. It was slow in the beginning, but that gave me time to spend with God for more and more direction from Him. I wanted to start just before school so I could still do legal work during the day, but God had other plans. When I sent out the flyer, I got very few requests for before and after school, but I got requests for a couple of full time younger kids. So in September 2008 I started full-time care with James and Miranda before school only.

It got off to a somewhat slow start, thanks to my getting in the way of God's working. I figured it would be good to finish off the few Guardian ad Litem cases I had left as a supplement to my income as I was getting started and as a just-in-case type thing.

Finally, after a series of events, I closed all my cases fully on an afternoon in December 2008. That night I got a call for twin infant boys to start immediately. The funny part is this person had my number since October and just hadn't called. She just happened to call the exact day I had finally fully let go of the law practice. Then God worked his magic and, by September of 2009, there were six to eight kids running around. Looking back I would say that I learned that, if we follow God's direction, He will provide what we need to be successful, but, too often, we get in the way with our 'better' plans.

I have been so blessed with that decision ever since I followed God. I have come to know and work with, and been able to pray for so many wonderful children, parents, and employees too. Sue Aschenbrenner, my employee and now friend, has made my return trips to Kenya possible. She is so trustworthy and reliable and does such a great job with the kids, I never worry about them or the business while I'm gone. She does a wonderful job... another miracle God has provided.

All this still left me wondering, "So now what?"

2

JULY 2009

NOW WHAT?

At this point, I was seeing more evidence in my life in so many ways, that God was working, yet I was still hesitant to label it that way for fear of turning into one of those 'churchie' people.

STARTING A NEW JOURNEY HERE

A couple of friends I met from the 2008 trip joked about having to go around the world to meet people who lived next door to us. Kristen, Pat, and I became close friends and committed to a Bible study group a few months after we returned. We had the wonderfully knowledgeable and inspiring woman, Pat Molitor to help us, the newbies, learn more about God. This study experience had a great impact on all of our lives. Working together to learn, God brought our lives back from despair in so many ways. We learned to deal with relationships; how to eat right; how cleaning the house could be a good way to relate to God, a better way to parent, and to do what God directed, no matter how difficult. The stories that came out of that study group could fill a book.

Many life-changing decisions came out of those weekly meetings. We would talk about our struggles and successes and look for answers by reading the Bible together. It was mind-boggling that a book so old, written by men so long ago, could actually address something in present times. I don't get it, and can't explain it, but somehow, it did.

We kept one another accountable for what we knew God wanted us to do in our lives, and came alongside each other to make these things happen. We met for years and continue to meet, though the people in the group, other than Pat and me, have changed over the years. Kristen moved to Kenya a few times and got married. Others joined for specific studies, and then left. Even my employees joined us at times. We still meet during the day, with the day care kids around us, listening and learning with us as we talk, laugh, and cry.

During this time, I also found a new radio station that helped me so much. I would listen to K-love all the time. It was on in the background at the day care center, all day long. It made the day go faster. It kept positive messages in my head instead of my own negative self-talk. The music was just so calming and peaceful and great. I remember a few moments when I had no strength or energy to do anything, and didn't think I could go on, a song would come on that would show me exactly what I was really struggling with so I could let it go and move on free. I am so grateful to K-love for playing the music that has made such a difference in my life in times when I really needed it. I love supporting them every month.

AGAIN

I was able to return to Kenya a year later, in July 2009, this time with my husband, Chris Reichartz. We got married the previous December, and Chris came even though he was on crutches. He was preparing for a half marathon and the stress from the preparation led to a broken lower leg.

Nevertheless it was great to experience Kenya with him.

Chris' biggest take-away from the trip was the fact that the food they eat and serve is not processed like our food. It is harder and a lot less sweet. We have so many chemical substances that we use here in the States, to keep our food really moist for a long time; but they don't use those things in Kenya, so food tastes a lot different. It is a lot healthier for you, and makes it a bit scary to think about all the things we constantly fill our bodies with here in America, that are not natural or healthy.

I am so grateful God gave me Chris. He is a wonderful husband, and if it was not for his support, I would not be able to do the things I am doing now. He contributes so much to the mission. He has donated time – rummage sales, paperwork, and other things – and money – supporting kids and donating in so many other ways. He is very understanding and supportive of my trips to Africa and helps ensure my kids here at home are accounted for while I'm gone. He drives me to the airport and usually picks me up with a few cold Diet Cokes stashed in a cooler. (I love Diet Coke and find it hard to live without, but Kenya does not have the luxury of this soft drink, so Chris always brings a few to me right when I get home. That's just one example of the many things he does to help me and encourage me.)

One of his other big take-aways was the fact that they recycle and reuse, or repurpose everything in Kenya. He does that a lot at home too and was surprised to see how much more they do it there. They do not throw anything away. They fix it, or reuse it in another way, to give 'waste' a new purpose.

I was able to connect with a few teenagers in Kenya last year, and was able to meet up with them again this year, and introduce them to Chris. Kennedy and Mercy are ones who come to mind. I had met Mercy the previous year, and then she found me in the huge crowd at the Vipingo Outreach Day. It was then that Mercy gave me the best present I have ever received. She brought me a woven basket that her grandmother had made for me. Knowing how little they have, and she has a lot of brothers and sisters so money is very tight, they wanted to bless me with this basket. To this day this basket graces my desk at home. I have since sold a lot of the items that I have picked up in Kenya as I would rather have the money to donate to Kenyan missions than Kenyan things that simply decorate my house; but this is one piece that will never leave.

It is great to continue to further friendships with some of the people I had met the year before. I was beginning to remember the names and faces of some staff and teachers, and came to learn more about them, including Rashid, our driver for the last few years. He has an engaging personality and is a wonderfully skillful driver.

Knowing that every part of the itinerary was drawing us closer and closer to the end made it difficult to stay in the moment and enjoy it. Nevertheless, God definitely renewed my passion for Kenya, although I had no idea where He was calling me to serve. Tears were part of a trip that went by way too fast. Again, it was very hard to leave and come home. I wanted to stay. If I had my way, I would live there. It was terribly difficult to leave Kenya not knowing whether God would lead me back the next year or ever.

RETURNING HOME

Once we returned to the States, I became really sick. I had a stomach infection from some of the food on the safari that I had cooked myself in the dark; which had not been fully cooked. Luckily for me, and everyone else on the plane, the infection didn't start until I touched down at Mitchell Airport and after I had located my luggage! Once I finally made it to the ER, days after I arrived home (having thought it would just go away), the health department quarantined me. I had to close the day care for a day – hopefully for the first and last time. I also struggled with the thoughts that my blood clot was again returning.

This was all too severe for me at the time, and I had moments that led me to say, "I am never going back; this is just too hard. I'm tired of it taking days and months to recover from the trip… then the blood clot, and now my stomach. I can't do it anymore." These things, in addition to the expense, made it seem more profitable for me to spend the money in the mission on the projects that had already been started. But I was soon to learn that in my weakness, God could shine.

Though I prayed prior to my trips to Kenya, I would not consider myself a good prayer. "God help my daughter to be safe. Help my son do well in school. Be with my friend in this difficult time."

In our weekly study, we started studying *Experiencing God* by Henry Blackaby. It was a life-changing study. It helped lay out steps to ensure and help people follow God's plan for their life. While reading the book and looking back on my life, and looking around me for God at work in my life, I noted several things, but nothing seemed to be coming together. He instructs in the book, "Just keep praying and looking for God to bring things in front of you. Most importantly, be open to seeing anything and everything God puts in front of you, not just your preconceived notion of what you think God should put in front of you". I was praying for direction about school decisions for my kids and, yes, for Kenya.

During the fall of 2009, I knew there was something going on concerning adoption in my life, but I didn't know what that meant. Fox River had done an adoption event for children in the Philippines that encouraged people to see the kids who were available for adoption, who were getting close to the age where they were too old to be adopted out. The subject interested me.

There were a few other ways that adoption had come across my path that month as well.

Adoption was always a big part of my life. My aunt, Karen, bless her heart, did foster care all her life and I loved helping her and being a very small part of what she did. She adopted five kids over the years and took in many, many more foster children. I always looked up to her and the work she did. In fact, I had gotten into law school mostly because of the essay I wrote about her work and my desire to be a Guardian ad Litem for kids in the system. (It certainly wasn't my B-/C+ grades in undergrad that got me in.)

At the same time some changes were happening in my child care business that not only provided a lot of free time for me, but also kept me wondering where God was leading. In the fall, the day care was just about full and doing great. Then, all of a sudden, we lost three kids in one weekend due to unemployment of the parents, and another had just started an extended two-month vacation period. That left us with two part-time children.

I had two employees at the time and could not keep both of them on board with that cut in income. I wasn't even sure if God wanted the day care to continue as He had opened up some leads for getting back into law in the area of child care regulations. There were lots of decisions to be made, and they were not only affecting me and the rest of my life, but other people and their children.

God worked it out, as usual. The employee I would have kept, as she was hired first, resigned via email taking another position that was to start immediately. I kept my one remaining employee's hours consistent out of fairness to her. While she was there, I was in intense prayer, asking God for direction on the day care center, direction on Kenya, direction with my kids, direction on life.

I tried whatever I could to find peace, purpose, and direction. I was committed to staying with this process as long as it took. I read the Bible. I kept a journal, although it was something I never liked doing. I developed a new journaling technique that really worked for me. Since I needed direction on three areas of my life, I divided the paper into four sections and wrote on the top of each section the area I wanted direction on, and then I listed below it the questions I had about that particular area. This process is what actually brought separate areas of my life together later on.

Here's an example of what I wrote in my journal while I was searching for direction at this time:

KENYA *Why do I keep going to Kenya? If I don't have a purpose there don't send me. It's money that could be donated.*	ADOPTION *Why does adoption seem to keep coming up all around me?*
KIDS' SCHOOL DECISION *Home school* *Online school* *What school*	OPEN BOX (List miscellaneous things that come up) *What do all these things mean?* *How does this all fit together?*

This was definitely new to me. In the past, I would merely ask my family and friends for their opinions and make a decision based on their consensus and what I wanted. To sit in silence, in hope and prayer, was new and scary. It felt like I was 'wasting' time doing nothing.

Little by little, as time passed, I began to see tremendous results and realized a lot more calm and peace in my life than ever before. After all this, God, brought me to tears with gratitude that He had given me the chance to go to Kenya, not once but twice. After this prayer and journaling, I heard two words spoken in my heart.

I was ecstatic. I finally had my purpose. Although I don't totally know what that meant by any means whatsoever, I had a 'Word'.

I had spent all that time praying and asking why God was sending me to Kenya and back again. The process took about a month… praying and journaling every afternoon for a few hours, God finally made the connection for me, after what felt like ten years (which was actually only months). Now I had it – direction. But that led to a lot more questions. It led to humbling phone calls to Bethany Christian Services and others, not knowing what God exactly meant by 'adoption'. It led to a lot of research on adoption in Kenya which was not very promising, though I learned a lot. Of course, I assumed it meant international adoptions. I did some random searches on adoption and international adoption. I did a lot of research about international adoption in Kenya, adoption agencies in Kenya, and the process of international adoption.

I ran into an organization called Little Angels Adoption Network, which, as it turns out, is the most well-known and used adoption agency in Kenya. It was started by a group of Christian women wanting to make a difference for kids in Kenya.

I also spent a lot of time on the US State Department website that outlined information about international adoptions. I was very disappointed by some of the information I found on Kenya. First, the US was not processing visas for Kenyan children, so they were not allowing adoptions at all at that point on the US side. But, on the Kenyan law side there is a mandatory stay of at least three months within the country if anyone wanted to adopt a child in Kenya. That lead me to immediately write a letter to the Kenyan Government telling them they were making it impossible for people to help them help their children. We cannot afford to leave here and live there for that long a time, outlining all the financial expenses as well as relationships and other things that would disrupt life in general.

I sent the letter to a few friends of mine for editing. My friend Erica Brobofsky indicated a few things that lead to the first step in a long journey of God's teaching me to come alongside and not to judge. I needed to find out why they have the rules they do, and work alongside in any way they might need to bring change to this process. They may ask for advice or they may not, but I need come alongside them anyway. I'm sure glad I learned that before I sent the letter off.

But, I was soon to learn how difficult it would be to stay focused, even with a 'Word'.

3

JULY 2010

CONNECTING THE DOTS

After the second trip, I did some serious soul searching about returning to Kenya. These trips are expensive and I questioned whether to donate the cost of US$3,500 to the kids of Kenya rather than spending it on travel.

I didn't see any purpose in my returning again. However, God eventually led me back to Kenya, this time taking Brooklyn, my 13-year-old daughter, along with me.

We saved for a year, beginning in September, 2009. My years seem to start based on when I arrive in Kenya! The calendar is of no value to me. Years are calculated in my head, Kenya trip to Kenya trip. Working in day care and trying to raise US$9,000 for two people to stay for three weeks in Kenya was not an easy task, but, with God's help, it worked out. We collected cans, sacrificed things like haircuts and other things to save what we could; hosted rummages, took things to resale shops, and put all extra monies and pocket change in the 'Kenya' jar in our kitchen to help keep us focused on the task. Through it all, God accomplished the goal.

BACK AGAIN

The first two weeks in Kenya were unchanged from prior years, working with the kids at Fox River's schools. It was particularly special to share these experiences with my daughter, who is so much like me (for better and for worse at times). My role was much different that year. I had much more of an administrative role; assisting with activities and helping those on their first trip to enjoy their new experience. At first, I didn't like being a leader. It meant I didn't get to interact as closely as I wanted to with the kids; but God and I had a 'mirror moment.' It seems that God talks to me a lot in Kenya while I'm standing in front of the mirror in the bathroom at the hotel. In this particular 'mirror moment,' God explained that this is what day-to-day life was like in Kenya and, if that is where I was to be, then these were the tasks I would be doing. From that point on I took the job with Godly purpose and no complaints.

The administrative role actually had some benefits to it. I was able to talk with the people in charge of the school and learn more about the kids and their lives at home.

I learned that most kids only eat when they are at school. When they go home, the little food that is at home is given to the other children in the family (who don't go to school) so they can stay as healthy as possible as this child (the one at school) is getting completely healthy meals at least five days. So the school meals not only giving this student a benefit, but the children at home, who are not in the schools, end up with more because this child is in the school. Though everyone wants to be in the school, there does not appear to be any jealously of kids that are in the school. The other kids are just grateful someone in their family has a chance to get an education and healthy food. The whole community, including all the kids, are thankful for the fresh water wells that Fox River provides for the local communities.

We also got a peak into how kids are chosen to enter these schools. As you can imagine – since this is the only truly 'free' school in the area – there are a lot of applicants for very few spots. We can only accept 34 students at each school.

Unfortunately there are hundreds of kids in these communities that need a chance at schooling. The way it works is that there is an application that the parents need to fill out (with our help if necessary) with basic information as well as financial information. For acceptance, they have to consider graphical location, age, as well as a gender balance when choosing the new classes.

Once applications are received (and they usually receive 160 of them each year), to fill 34 spots, the applications are reviewed by a quite few people. If applicants have *any* level of income they are generally rejected. (In these areas of Kenya, to make US$30 or more a month is considered middle class!) If they make the financial, gender, age and location cut, then the medical records for the children are examined for a health check. Once the health checks are complete, the kids who are the sickest are chosen for the school. Usually the sickness steams from starvation.

This is yet another sad reality of life in Kenya.

I thank God for the people who make these decisions, as hard as they are to make. I have learned so much from Denise Conn, the mission director at our church. We have to follow what God calls us to, and be specific and intentional about these calls. For example, if God calls us to feed all at Vipingo, we need to do just this, and not schools and food. But if God calls us to 'do' schools and feed, we cannot only chose to start a school or simply feed kids. In the same way, if God calls us to limit our scope, we need to do that or it will no longer have God's full blessing upon it.

Small class sizes produce quality education for these children. We cannot let everyone into the school, because the standards of education and amount of nutritional food available would be compromised. This is not an easy reality, but we have to remain content with what God calls us to do. We also need to pray and come alongside others as they come to do what God has called them to do. It is tempting to think, "God this is making such a small difference in this huge world, why even do it?" Then we need to think about the huge difference it is making in the lives of each of the 350 kids, their families and communities; how these efforts will be touching them year after year, once the classes are full up to Grade 8.

The third week was different from other times I had spent in Kenya. My friend Luann and daughter Nora, Rosie and her son Jordan, and Brooklyn and I were termed the Kenya 6.

We were the six who were staying behind after the rest of the group had left. We had all been to Kenya before (except for Brooklyn) and knew what to expect. We had some ideas about extra activities we would like to try that would benefit the communities around the Fox River schools. We thought we could handle these as a small group. We knew the experiences would be new to us, however, there was no way I could have prepared for what was in store.

Things happened very quickly. That's how God works sometimes.

RELATIONSHIP CONNECTIONS

On Pastor Paul's prompting, we organized an outreach initiative to teenagers in Vipingo. We played some team-building games and conducted a written activity that got them thinking about their futures and positive things to focus on instead of alcohol, sex, and other common teenage negative activities. School was a recurring difficulty and stress for them.

I remembered a favorite activity I did at Girl Scout camp as a teen. So we had the Kenyan teens perform skits about various topics. First, we assigned the topics: sex, drugs, responsibility, and alcohol. Then we had miscellaneous items from our luggage, and laid them out, and the kids had to choose ten items to incorporate into their skit in some way and every item had to be used.

They had one hour to make up a skit. After this, they presented it to the group. The skits were great and the kids did a good job and had a fun time doing it. We ended the day with a big lunch provided by Fox River. I hope it was a good learning experience for the teens from Vipingo. Though we were nervous about the teen day, it turned out to be one of the best days of the week.

All day, a boy with Down's Syndrome was hanging around the school and church as we had the teen activities. His name was Henzie. He was a cute child, respectful, and polite. He wore a tattered shirt. He asked, without words because he was unable to speak, if he could have lunch with us. Since we had plenty of leftovers, we welcomed him. He ate more than I could ever eat. We found a new shirt for him, too, but he insisted on wearing his old tattered one over it. I'm sure he wanted to make sure he took it home for repurposing.

The head teacher at that school, Paul Odhiambo, decided to find out more about the boy. Apparently, Henzie was being left home alone every day because both of his parents worked and he was not getting enough to eat. Now he is at the school and eating with them every day. The school is attempting to find ways to teach him in ways he can learn with guidance of special education teachers within Fox River.

This was yet another success story for the community of Vipingo, and Henzie and his family.

On another day, we went into the community to help a family rebuild their mud-hut kitchen that had been washed away by flooding earlier in the year. Building even part of a mud hut is quite a process. Luckily, we had Teddy, a 13-year-old, long-time Vipingo friend to assist. I think he was the only person accompanying us who had done this before. He demonstrated how it was done.

First, we had to dig a hole in order to make the mud, and then we had to loosen dirt to create the mud. We needed to get water, dump it in the hole, step into the hole, and knead the water and the dirt together to make mud with our feet. After this, we had to take some mud, and a large stone, and put these into a rectangular shape, one foot long by four inches tall. Then we had to start again. Run for water, find more stones, make more mud, and, slowly, assemble a hut. It was quite messy, but it was a lot of fun working alongside our Kenyan friends (Teddy, Nicole, and Paul) and our new friends (the homeowners). It took us about two hours to complete the task; a task the homeowner indicated would have taken him three days or more. He was very grateful for the help.

When we arrived, he had been very hesitant about us, and our offer to help. But by the time we left, he was asking for pictures with all of us in front of the hut, and was smiling from ear to ear.

Various Kenyans commented that it touched the community that we were not just coming to look and take pictures and go home, but that we actually came alongside and helped them in their need. That made a difference, it made them feel not forgotten. The family was very grateful and we had a great time actually becoming one with the culture. It was an unforgettable experience. In fact, a few weeks after we got back to the States, we received a thank you note from the wife, with various 'thanksgiving' Bible verses. A week after that, we got word from Pastor Paul that the husband had been to church for the first time in several years. God was definitely at work, even in the messy mud.

Now that Fox River has been working in these villages for a few years, God has made some changes in the community. The kids and people in the community smile more. Every person in both of these communities (Vipingo and Bomani) has been touched in some way, largely through having their children in the schools and feeding them daily.

Church attendance has grown.

The wells that have been built have brought down the number of illnesses being reported to the Kenyan Public Health Department in these communities because they are now drinking, and using, clean water instead of dirty water.

Members of the community now come together once a year to have fun, celebrate life and eat together.

You can find some of the stories of community change outlined in Chapter 8, *Remember Me*. But there are so many more stories of personal life change that we will never know about. As long as they continue to see the love of God shining, I am happy.

GRATITUDE FOR BREAKFAST

One day, I was walking with Edgar and his friend Michael in the village. Edgar is a third-grader at our Vipingo school. Trying to make simple conversation, as language can be an issue, I asked him some questions. Finally, running low on ideas, I asked him, "What time do you leave for school in the morning?" It seemed like a harmless, simple question. He answered, "6 am". I said, "6 am, I thought school started at 8 am?" He replied, "It does". I said, "You walk two hours to school every morning?" He responded, without any burden or complaint, "Yes. Thank you for breakfast."

As an aside, during the past year, for US$20 a month, our church has started offering a very small cup of porridge breakfast to the kids so they have a good start in the morning to learn. Instead of complaining, even a little, for having to walk four hours a day to get to and from school, Edgar thanked me for his small cup of porridge. This was a very humbling learning experience for me. Often we complain about having to go to school and wouldn't even think of walking four hours for it. I complain about so much, from the weather to the fact that this or that isn't what I want it to be. I complain about 'starving' when I'm at home and haven't eaten in awhile. Meanwhile, this is a daily reality for people in Kenya and they go through it without complaint, even rejoicing in the little they have.

The Kenya 6 also went to Ingili (Gospel) in the village of Majaoni for church on Sunday. Brooklyn dressed in her African conga (a wrap-around skirt, but for Brooklyn, a dress) that she received from the generous staff at Bomani. She had it tied up in a way that looked so cute and so African, like a 'Masai Mamma,' according to a few Kenyans. It brought tears to my eyes to see the amount of love they have for God, and each other, when they have so little to be thankful for. I wish I was more like that. I wish my society was more like that.

As I write today, there is a downpour outside, but I don't worry about it; I know my house will withstand the hard rain. There is a small chance my basement could flood, but my dwelling will be in place without any thought or concern. In Kenya they worry their mud hut will wash away, leaving them without shelter and without money to purchase the materials necessary to rebuild. They sit under leaking roofs that have been thatched together with dried palm tree branches. I have clean running water at my constant disposal. They have to walk miles to get water and it is usually dirty water that makes them sick. Still, they are truly grateful to God for what they do have. It brings tears to my eyes to see them so happy, content, and full of praise despite the fact that they have very little to be happy about.

GOD CONNECTING THE DOTS

Several people from our church had returned to Kenya for several years. They seemed to have their passions all fall into place.

We have a teacher that does in-service trainings for the teachers while we are there. We have Rosie who has completed nursing school and the church is supporting her as she starts medical mission trips. I had been watching their passion for Kenya take effect and saw how the doors had really opened for them. They seemed to have such clear direction and vision. This led me to think, "Where do I belong?" I prayed, "I know you said adoption, God, but I don't see that happening." I don't know anyone who has adopted, is adopting, or has anything to do with adoption.

It is really hard to feel such a deep passion for something and not have any idea what the outlet for that passion should be, especially when that passion is halfway around the world!

After a ceremony at Bomani, a Fox River school, I had a talk with Rosie. We were talking about finding a niche, and talking with others. She encouraged me to talk with Allan, a pastor at Bomani, as he had many connections. I was very hesitant. The Kenyan accent is difficult to understand and fear stood in the way of my moving forward. Rosie finally pushed me enough and I hesitantly told Allan of my leaning toward adoption. Thanks to Allan, within a minute I was on the phone with a lawyer, whom Allan knew, who does adoption work. He was busy with some constitutional issues (they had a referendum the next day to vote on a constitution for their country), but he got us in touch with a lawyer friend of his, Vicky Nzoiki. We set up a time to come by and see her an hour later.

This is something that wouldn't happen in the States. There is a different attitude about time in Kenya. As a lawyer in the States, one's time is planned weeks, months, and years ahead and there's no time for last-minute appointments, especially ones like these. We simply don't make the time. Court systems in America schedule dates years out, while in Kenya the court dates schedule only two weeks out. That time difference can be a hindrance as well as a benefit. At first I thought of it as a hindrance. I had spent thousands of dollars to get to Kenya but I couldn't get anyone to commit to meetings until I got there. That's a lot of money spent months in advance with nothing confirmed. That used to stress me out, but now I have come to appreciate and even like the Kenyan way of going about business. Things can get accomplished in a day that would take years the American way. I have to trust God to set up the meetings and events and not myself. It's not an easy place for me to be, but I have learned a lot and am much more comfortable with it now.

One hour later, Allan was announcing/introducing me to Vicky. We had a general conversation about running a law office and adoption law. Vicky is an amazing person who does a lot of great work. She works on clean water projects, women and family issues, and human rights issues as a lawyer. She also belongs to law societies and community groups that are making a difference. At this meeting, we talked mostly about international adoption, as I still had no idea what God had in mind with this work. We talked about how the process could be streamlined and where in the process kinks could be worked out. We stayed in touch via email after that. During that conversation I thought God was leading me to return in October to further this work.

The meeting did not give me all the answers, but most of the things we discussed I had already learned a little about from the Internet when I did my initial search in December, January, and February. I felt that God had directed my Internet search and led me to this and was continuing to lead.

I am just along for the ride.

WAYS TO HELP

Things also came together concerning things I could do in the States to help. I spoke to the missionaries, Jim and Susie Horne who have been living in Kenya for over 30 years doing this work of planting churches and schools and feeding centers. I also talked with Bobby and Lisa Bechtel, missionaries doing the same thing, asking them how I could be most effective while asking for money and how I should go about it.

This gave me guidance and direction as I prepared to hit the ground looking for funds.

I also had time to brainstorm with a new missionary, Kristen, a friend of mine whom I had met on our first trip in 2008. Both of us had a deep desire to help a specific school that was suffering – Tiwi. I worked on getting the 501(c)(3) tax status from the IRS and other administrative tasks started in the States for both the missionary teams we are working with in Kenya.

Meanwhile, Kristen was already planning on being in Kenya for a year to get bios and photos of all the kids in Vipingo, Tiwi, Perani, and Tumaini (all the Operation Give Hope schools) and Ingili and Bomani (the Hope Foundation schools). Then the bios and photos were entered into two websites so sponsors here in the US or around the world could stay connected with their kids in Kenya while sponsoring their food and education for US$25 a month.

Operationgivehope.org (www.operationgivehope.org) and Operation Give Hope – Facebook and The Hope Foundation – Facebook and www.hopefoundation.co.ke were born.

HEADING HOME AGAIN

The last couple days were spent in Nairobi, Kenya's capital city.

This was my first time in Nairobi.

We saw an elephant orphanage, where kindly people take in baby elephants that had been orphaned because of poaching or abandonment.

We went to Kibera, the largest slum in Africa and walked around the streets there for a while, and visited a few school classrooms filled with kids.

We climbed a mountain (a very large hill) that almost took everything out of me, but I did it! I couldn't help but notice how out-of-shape I was. I had been a gymnastics coach for many years and always loved to work out. But when my blood clot started, the doctor and I thought it was a pulled calf muscle that stemmed from a workout I had on a treadmill that morning. That was not in fact the case; it was from a hormone in my birth control patch. But nonetheless, it was really hard for me, psychologically, to work out so I stopped and it really showed on this trip up the mountain.

We spent some time driving to see the Great Rift Valley we had all learned about in social studies. It was beautiful and gave us another perspective of Kenya.

Soon, the time to leave Africa approached (again). God kept my mind active on the way home this time, and something occurred to me that sounded so simple and cliché, but was so life-changing at the same time. Our whole lives are mission trips. I had to slow down for a minute and ponder that thought.

We are here on earth for a temporary period. Our real home is in heaven, if we have accepted Jesus. Therefore, every second of every day should be lived as though it is a mission trip. We are on a mission here on earth to love one another and teach others by our example. Are we living and spending our time and money as if that was true today?

47

Leaving this time was not so difficult. God had already provided the direction. I was to return to Kenya in October 2010 and this time He had already provided most of the funds through a generous donation of a friend. I had done some legal work for him and he made a very generous donation toward my Kenya travels.

After the 2010 trip my daughter didn't even want to return home, which is amazing for a 13-year-old without cell phone service and very sporadic Internet for three weeks.

I came back with a 'to do' list a mile long, starting with opening a non-profit organization, Operation Give Hope, and setting up an office. I was on fire and rearing to go. Though I would have loved to live in Kenya, I wasn't in that place yet. I now knew some things I could work on in the States to raise awareness of the issues and show people and churches what little it takes to allow God to make a huge difference. This brought me a lot of peace.

It took a long time to get back on a normal sleep schedule after the three-week trip. But I discovered that I am most productive right after I get back from Kenya. There is never another time I can accomplish so much in one day. I guess when you get up regularly at 2 am for a month, it leads to a lot of alone time to get work done without interruption because no one else is awake, except your online Kenyan friends. With this post-trip insomnia I wanted to get the office up and running and start organizing fund raising events for Tiwi, my favorite school and one that was in desperate need for funds. I would get up every morning with the intention of working on that.

But every morning God would lead me to, of all things, planning a teen mission trip to Kenya.

After returning from the trip in July 2010 with Brooklyn, a lot of her friends expressed an interest in going to Kenya the following year. God gave me the idea to start a teen weekly Bible study program in which we would meet weekly to discuss God and His Word and how it works in their lives... and brainstorm and carry out fund raisers to raise money for a mission trip.

The goal was to prepare the kids ,weekly to be emotionally ready by hearing stories from others who had taken the trip, and other kids their age who are making a real difference in the world.

The goal was to be spiritually ready by getting closer to God and getting to know Him better. Other goals were to become mentally ready by learning about Kenyan language, culture, and government, and to be financially ready by fund raising.

Although we had some great friends here and there joining in, at the end only one of Brooklyn's friends joined us on the full journey. Little did I know why God was so pushy about getting this started so quickly. I had been begging God to start this teen thing a year later.

Let's wait till the money is in place for Tiwi. "Let me focus on the other work you have begun to lead me to".

I prayed. I had a 'to do' list a mile long, but God kept getting me up at 2 am and led me to planning this teen trip... so I did it.

I scheduled an informational meeting in September and Josie, Brooklyn's best friend, and her mother came to hear more about it. Her mom was excited and offered to help in any way she could. We had a rummage sale in October that her mom helped with, and we sent letters out to area businesses asking for support. Her mom was able to get us all the addresses from a database she had.

In November, however, the unthinkable happened. Josie's mom passed away suddenly. The family was in crisis. God, through this Bible study group and my family, was able to reach out to Josie and her dad to help them through this difficult time. God had sent the right people. Brooklyn's dad had passed away a few years earlier just as suddenly. So we had been through this. We were the perfect fit to help this family through a difficult time. Josie had a woman figure to talk with if she needed, and more importantly she had a better understanding of God and how much He loved her. In addition, preparing for Kenya was the perfect way for her to keep focused forward as she readjusted to her new life.

But for now, I was going it alone in October 2010...

4

OCTOBER 2010

GOING IT ALONE

In October 2010, I returned to Kenya alone because it was more of a business trip. It started out on a less than positive note. My closest aunt, Karen, who molded a lot of my passions in life – adoption and kids – passed away right as my plane was taking off. I didn't know this until I arrived in Kenya. She had suffered from lung cancer and they had given her six months to live three years ago. We will miss her dearly. She had a great last few years traveling, and with time to say goodbye. Sadly, I missed the funeral. My mom and husband Chris would be there, but my kids would go to the funeral without me. The last funeral they had gone to was their dad's three years ago. It was a very sad start to the trip.

If it wasn't for my mom, these trips would not be possible. She is quite an example, giving the shirt off her back to anyone in need… and she'd help iron it first. She always volunteers to help in so many ways, often taking me with her. Now she was taking my kids with her. She donates time and money. She 'helps' (usually doing more than I do) me with rummages that I have at her house because she in a great location for rummages. She is always giving me things to take to Kenya for the kids. She takes care of, and watches over my kids while I'm gone. She makes sure homework is done and that they get to school on time, as well as to all their activities. She even helps out with the day care center once in a while for free, so I can get to meetings or other things I need to do. I owe a lot to my mom for making all of these things possible.

APPRECIATION FOR THE SCHOOL STAFF

Kenyan teachers, similar to those in the States, get paid less working in a private school than they would if they worked at a public school; so it is imperative that they buy into the mission as well as the paycheck, or we would have a high turn-over rate, which is not good for the children's learning or the school.

It's important to let them know how much their work is appreciated and to team build. This was the purpose of the first Staff Appreciation Day. The hope and motivation was to re-energize the staff by giving them some good food, playing fun games, and creating good memories. Fox River funded the event and Kristen and Paul implemented the ideas. Then we all prepared for the day. Staff from Ingili, Bomani, and Vipingo schools were invited, as well as staff from another school run by other missionaries in Mombasa, Chris and Lisa Moore.

The staff we had invited were so excited that they showed up an hour early, so most of them were there before Kristen and I arrived. (This is unheard of in Kenya, where people generally show up notoriously late.)

The event took place at a beautiful butterfly park, where there were nature trails and lots of different kinds of trees, not unlike a nicer State or County park in the States. It was extremely hot, even for the Kenyans.

Once all 90 people had arrived, we divided into ten teams. Each team had to come up with a name and create a logo for the team, using coins we provided. It was fun to watch their imaginations at work. Then they headed off to the nature trail/ exercise course for a scavenger hunt. They had a lot of fun on the trails interacting and getting to know their team members better. When we returned, I read a letter from Pastor Guy Conn, the senior pastor at Fox River Christian Church in the US, encouraging them. Then Bobby, the missionary from Bomani, gave a sermon about working together and valuing everyone's job. We mingled while eating lunch and then played a few more games.

Then the day was complete.

REALITY HITS AGAIN – SACRIFICE?

As the staff left, we heard many comments about how they would never forget this day, and how very special it had been for them. Some indicated, with tears in their eyes, that this was the best day of their lives.

In the States, we organize days like this a lot, and we take them for granted. In fact a lot of the time we come up with excuses to get out of work picnics, while here it was a day they would NEVER forget. That was very sobering and it made me cry.

The staff passed along well wishes and gratitude for the sacrifices that we in America do to pay their salaries and to support the schools. The US$20 per month per student that sponsors provide covers all expenses of the school: salaries, books, uniforms, food, and the rest. So often, the teachers thank me for the sacrifice I am making to support the school.

At this time, I was supporting about five kids from the school and really, that was not a sacrifice. I could handle this amount without changing my lifestyle much.

If I was being completely honest, sending that amount each month did not affect my life much at all. On the rare occasion when things did get tight financially, the only thing I did have to cut back on was going through the drive-thrus, which was at times a major downfall for me. For some, it's their coffee money, eating out at lunch, having a few drinks at the bar which can be very expensive; we all have something that is not really even good for us and we spend a lot of money to do it. Giving something like this up is all it takes to change so many lives. God has had me on a journey of learning about what true sacrifice is, and at this point in my journey I was not yet there.

When I would think about what the money was going towards, and not on what I was giving up, it was a lot easier to make it a priority. It's harder to say to myself, "You cannot eat at McDonalds at all this month so you can give the money you would spend to a deserving cause". Instead it is easier for me to say, "If I send money to Kenya this month, a child will eat two meals a day and get to go to school instead of being left in a cycle of poverty – is my McDonalds' meal worth that much to me?".

Now, I give more, and it is one of the first things I take care of every month because it was the most important 'bill' to me. And while I've been doing that, I have come to realize there is never a month when the rest of my bills don't get paid. God seems to take care of it, even if my income drops unexpectedly for some reason.

CONNECTING KENYA AND THE WORLD

Kristen and I worked on collecting the bios and photographs of all the kids from all the Operation Give Hope schools – Vipingo, Perani, Tiwi, and Tumaini. While we were there, we took photos, recorded the height and weight of all the children, and did a medical examination. There were 1,500 children in all that Kristen compiled information for. Everything went very well and we got it done in record time, thanks to all the helpful teachers and Kristen's organizational skills. It was great to spend some time at lunch with the younger children at the school and also to see how faces have changed over the years.

Now we needed to upload the data we had obtained from all the kids over the past several weeks onto the Internet, so that when people wanted to sponsor kids, they could go onto the website to learn more about the children and their families, living conditions, their favorite subjects and activities, where they live and what is going on with them in school.

We knew it would be a great resource, but a lot of typing was needed to get it together. However, with all that we were trying to accomplish, we worked from 6 am until midnight every day, yet somehow still had enough energy to keep going. At home, I go to bed at 9 pm and get up at 5 am. This trip was definitely sailing on God's strength, being out of my routine and comfort.

I did, however, have a lot of this work to take home with me. This meant I had to spend a day making photocopies and getting things organized to prepare for working at home. We were also typing up labels to put on the back of the Kenya school-kid photos for Fox River's *My Gift for Jesus* campaign this year. There is a table in the gym where people can come and look at all the school kids' photos and choose one who grabs their heart to sponsor. This way the sponsors will know more about the kids on the photo itself, as well as where to go to get more information. Fox River sets this up for a few weeks, starting the weekend after Thanksgiving every year. I wonder how much could be accomplished if every church did this, even for one week a year. How much money could we raise for Jesus' birthday if we all joined together and encouraged one another? It gives new meaning to the phrase, "Reason for the Season" doesn't it?

What are you planning on giving Jesus for his birthday this year?

STRANGER DANGER PRESENTATIONS

Pastor Allan, the pastor who helped Fox River get Bomani started, said that it was mentioned on television that about 144,000 kids had been abducted in Kenya since March of 2010. Apparently, witch doctors pay a lot of money for human – especially children's – body parts. Abducted kids had been found dead and with body parts cut off. Please take a moment to pray for these communities, to keep their children safe.

Given the situation in Kenya, the missionaries we work with at Bomani school, Bobby and Lisa Bechtel, asked me if I could do a 'stranger danger' presentation to the kids at Tiwi, Bomani, Vipingo, and Ingili.

We did a short interactive session with the kids. We talked about staying on the main pathways when traveling, staying in a group, walking with an adult, running away from people they don't recognize if they are by themselves, and a few other preventative things. We started talking about what to do if someone did attempt to grab them. First, we taught them how to scream, and we practiced a few times. It took a while to get them to actually do it because they are naturally very quiet kids in school. They are taught respect and manners and they are afraid to scream or make a fuss. But after a few tries they finally were shouting. Then we talked about kicking, hitting, and biting if necessary, all the while screaming and trying to run away.

We then had some time for questions. One of the girls asked, "You told us to bite if we needed to get away, what if the person grabbing us has HIV, won't that cause us to get HIV?" It was another reality check; things here are not the same.

In Kenya it is assumed that everyone is HIV positive, whereas in the States HIV is the exception to the rule, rather than the norm. I hope God will use this lesson to help anyone who needs it and will keep these kids safe from harm.

SOUTH COAST - TIWI

I was up at 5 am so we could make it through the downtown area without encountering heavy traffic and so we would not have to wait hours to get across on the car ferry to get to the south coast. This is a typical south coast morning. It is wise to get up early to avoid any potential major delay – hours and hours of sitting in your car waiting for traffic.

I deeply love the south coast. It's where I fell in love with Kenya for the first time. In Tiwi in 2008, I had met a young girl, who, at that time, was in KG-2 and was so quiet she would not even tell me her name without whispering. I had to ask Pastor Vincent, who oversees Tiwi, what her name was. She was so cute; a small child with braids in her hair. I watched her from afar for a little while and then moved closer until she came over to sit on my lap. Her name was Mwanarose, and she was doing a really good job in school, and was very advanced in her classes (she still is).

Now, every time I go there, it's interesting to see how much she's grown. Even just the second year I saw her, when she was in KG-3, she was already on stage yelling out a poem as a presentation in English. At this grade, it is still difficult for students to speak English. I have since learned that Mwanarose is the youngest in her family and she has three older brothers. Her dad is a teacher, but not at our school. Her mother passed away in 2010. Every time I saw her I noticed that she wore the same ripped and tattered shirt under her uniform. Finally, in March 2012, I went to Good Will and bought her a few outfits. When they called her from class to the office to get the gift, the outfits were laid out on a desk so she could see them. She was quite surprised and couldn't believe that she could have so many choices in what to wear. She didn't think they were all for her.

This is another luxury that most of us take for granted, without even thinking about the fact that so many people in the rest of the world don't even have adequate clothing. I hope to visit her house on a future visit. She lives very close to the Tiwi property, and her grandmother lives with her to help her dad care for the kids. She has one brother in high school and another brother in 8th grade who is very bright. Her second oldest brother had the highest score in the entire district in 2011, on the very important 8th grade standardized exam. That is amazing and a tremendous compliment to him and to the staff at Tiwi Baptist Academy.

SOUTH COAST - PERANI

Baraka Baptist Academy, located in Perani, Kenya, is a school that is approximately one-and-a-half hours from Tiwi (which is already one to two hours from Mombasa, where we were staying). Pastor Daniel is in charge of that school and is a wonderful man.

This was my first, and so far has been my only visit to this school. It was great to see another school and compare it to the Fox River schools. It makes such a difference in the culture when a church is 100 percent behind the school. One can see the difference, not only in the physical appearance of the school and the books and other things at the school, but more importantly, one can see the difference in the eyes of the children. When the children see the hands and feet of God coming to visit them every year, knowing how much they are loved and cared for, their eyes reflect more hope, and positive energy flows through.

Through the work of Jim and Susie Horne, who have been missionaries in Mombasa, Kenya for more than 30 years, as well as the work Kristen has done, and the work I will do at home, with God's blessing, we will hopefully be able to get this school and the second school we saw that day, fully sponsored by a church.

SOUTH COAST - TUAMINI

Mwangda is where a little school called Tumaini has started. Tumaini is not far from Perani, and back towards Tiwi. Pastor Steven and his wife Monica have started this school, but it is heartbreaking.

When we went there we were taking pictures and asking the kids to laugh and smile, but they couldn't. There was very little, if any, hope in their eyes. They looked tired and worn out.

The school consists of a few mud huts that Pastor Steven and his wife had built. Their baby classroom for 35 kids is the size of my closet (maybe 9 ft x 9 ft) and it has no roof because they cannot afford the 1,000 schillings (approximately US$12.00) to put a roof on it. The kids sit in this tiny classroom with the extremely hot equatorial sun beating down on them for hours. At the church, they are praying for a roof. The only touch of hope at that school resides with the great teachers, Joseph, Johnson, John, the women teachers, and Pastor Steve who is in charge of the school and six churches in the outlying area. He has each school teacher take one church a week and follows them to make sure everyone in the community can reach the church to get fed by the word of God.

The worst part for this community is their water situation. Earlier that year they had NO water (clean or dirty). In May and June they'd had a lot of rain, and as a result they had, literally, a pond with yellow and green lily pads to drink out of. The teachers and Pastor Steve told us there was sewage waste in the water, but they were just so grateful to at least have some water in the community. It was truly heartbreaking. They hoped the pond would last for two to three years, but when Kristen visited soon afterwards, the level had already dropped a lot. To make matters even worse, there were three crocodiles living in the water. This was a place where little ones went to fetch water for their families, with even littler ones on their back. This was not a safe situation in so many ways, yet they praised God for that water. It was dirty sewer water with crocodiles in it, but it was water.

It's completely heartbreaking and gives one a lot of perspective. I couldn't help but cry on the way back from Tumaini, thinking about how grateful to God they were for dirty water while I am able to sit at home and buy pretty much anything I want, and eat anything I want, and drink anything I want without thought.

A LAWYER AGAIN, FOR A DAY AT LEAST

I spent a day at the Mombasa courthouses with Vicky. We had a chance to see the municipal, county, and some federal-level courts in action. We watched some court appearances and mingled with the lawyers waiting for their cases to be called out in the hallways.

Vicky had a big civil rights case for women that day. Police were unfairly targeting women to prosecute for certain sex crimes and, under the 'new' constitution, that is illegal. Vicky brought one woman's case in a suit against various governmental agencies. It was a really big case. Unfortunately, her case was delayed, but I left the courthouse praying it would go well for all the parties involved.

Then at the end of the day, we sat in on a first ever video conference court appearance between Mombasa and Nairobi for the Court of Appeals. After being in court for a few days, and meeting many lawyers, I remembered how much I missed practicing law. I enjoy what I am doing in the day care industry, but I also miss the relationships and small talk between lawyers and judges.

THE START OF SOMETHING

Vicky introduced me to Hellen Macharia, a psychologist who works with Little Angels Adoption Network (an organization that places kids from orphanages in Kenya into adoptive homes).

We discussed the problems she sees in the adoption process in Kenya both domestically and internationally. We talked about possible solutions and the reasons why Kenyan laws had become what they were. We discussed whether there were other ways to address these issues, and how we could address some of the problems.

Hellen has a great passion for adoption. She has even adopted children herself. She said that she saw two problems standing in the way of adoption, moving forward in Kenya, that needed to be addressed.

Firstly, adoption at this time was a new thing in Kenya – only ten years old – and people didn't understand it. They would see the children in orphanages, but didn't understand that they were available to be brought home and into their own families. People will do their good deed by visiting the children and then going home. Even educated people, psychologists and lawyers, didn't understand that it is in the best interest of these kids to grow up in a family and not an institution. The process was new and not widely known.

Secondly, people who do adopt are generally shunned by family and community members. There is a stigma that people have 'bought' a child, or that they should rather take care of their own cousin's baby whom they cannot afford to take care of, not reach out to 'buy' a baby. That brought to light an important need that had to be met, but I didn't think much about it at the time.

MEETINGS, MEETINGS, MEETINGS

Remarkably, Pastor Allan was able to organize a few different meetings with various people in Nairobi who work in the courts and government. They gave us great advice, encouragement, and hope. They fully supported our efforts with the schools as well as the adoption issues.

One of the meetings was with the head of the Kenyan Lawyers Society. I talked with him about the possibility of getting a Kenyan law license. I had been praying for that to come to fruition on this trip. However, the lawyer strongly discouraged my pursuit of the license.

Through that conversation and journaling, God showed me that He didn't want me to be on anyone's side, despite the fact that I have both a law degree in the US and an undergraduate degree in psychology. God made it clear to me that He wants me to be a liaison between the two professions in order to come together for the kids in adoption, not on one side more than the other.

Though I am disappointed about not pursuing a law license in Kenya, at least for now, I know this is God's project not mine and it will all work out His way, which is just fine with me whatever the outcome.

We met at the Hotel Serena, which was the same hotel where they had settled the violence issues around the election in 2008; and had decided on shared government, and on passing the constitution which they did in August 2010. Those were some powerful workings of God, from total chaos and violence two years before, to forming a new constitution and governmental protections. It was a new beginning for the government and people of Kenya.

Only God can bring such newness out of such darkness.

During this trip, I began what would evolve into this book. With Kristen's encouragement, I created an Internet blog, as others at home had wanted to keep up with what was going on in Kenya. I didn't realize how God would use that blog to touch so many people and to lead me. In my blog posts I would simply outline what we had done that day, who we had spoken with, where we had gone; not much more than that at the beginning.

Within hours of posting the first entry regarding working on adoption issues in Kenya, I was contacted by a Kenyan girl on Facebook. She was pregnant and didn't know where to turn. She was afraid of being kicked out of her house for being pregnant, and didn't know how she would be able to continue in school. I had the same situation in my life while I was in college, so I could relate not only to the problem, but to her feelings as well. I was able to help get her in contact with some people who would be able to help her through this difficult situation. I also prayed with her, through Facebook, whenever she needed.

That was my first sign that there was a need for a pregnancy crisis center in Kenya. I had further discussions with pastors, lawyers, and social workers about the need. No pregnancy crisis center exists in Mombasa. There is one agency people can call, but it is a place where they help you find places to have illegal abortions, not offer to help any other solutions. There is no emotional help for girls in that situation.

This is the path God has led me on for so many reasons.

ASKING FOR HELP

As I left, I was not exactly sure when I would return to Kenya. I was hoping to go back in the spring of 2011, but if not, in summer that year, with my daughter and her friend Josie.

While at home, God led me to fund raising. I don't consider myself good at this. One way God has led me is to organize run/walks. I hate running and avoid it like the plague, so I don't even have experience doing a run/walk let alone planning one. I will need a lot of help. One of my major problems with fund raising in general, and through all of life in so many ways, is that I don't like to ask for help. I would rather merely work harder and do it myself than to have to ask someone for help. However, with a task like this and others God is leading me into, I need to ask for assistance all the time.

A radio station that I love to listen to, K-love, had a great idea. They were talking about picking a *Word for the Year*. Pick one word that would be something you would focus on for the coming year. Read books on the topic, or just watch your life in that area and see how it develops through the year. I thought that was an interesting idea, so in 2011, I picked the word 'ASK.' Knowing that I was not very good at asking for help or asking for things I thought this would be a challenge. That year brought me a lot further in that journey, and left me feeling a lot more comfortable about asking. "People can always say no, but I can at least ask", is my new motto. It has brought many small and large miracles into my life and has expanded my work and my life.

It's actually rather amusing. God knows that I hate asking for help, yet He called me to work in Kenya, 14,000 miles away from home, where I knew very few people and I couldn't do anything for myself. I still need a ride everywhere; I need help setting up meetings; and so many other things. It is not safe for me to travel alone without a Kenyan... (and it should be a Kenyan man) with me most of the time. Yet God sets it up so I need to ask for help for EVERYTHING. God truly has a great sense of humor doesn't He? Needless to say, I'm getting much better at asking for help.

When I got home we continued the teen Bible study group with Brooklyn, Josie, and friends. We met weekly, learning about Kenya and managing various fund raising projects. In our weekly meetings we learned about who God is, who we are in Christ, that we are beautiful, loved, free, and so many other things.

We continued to use the Bible to help us find new perspective and solve our problems in life. Every week we would come up with an area that we were struggling with. It might be loneliness, sadness, feeling ugly, or something else. Once each person picked their own topic for the week, we used either a computer at Biblegateway.com or a concordance (a listing of topics) to find verses that would help us in that area. For example, if someone struggled with loneliness, we would type that or lonely into Biblegateway.com "topic box" and it would pull all verses with loneliness or lonely in them. Or we would look up the word lonely or lonelieness in the concordance list. Then once we had a list of verses, we would read through them, then choose one, and write it out on an index card that we would tape to a place where we would read it often and then talk about how the verse was helpful at the next meeting.

It's funny, because I didn't kid myself and think the girls were studying these verses daily. In fact, I know most of the weeks the cards never left their binders; yet when we talked about our week the next week, the girls could see how their life had changed in that area, simply writing that verse down and never putting any more thought into it until the next week. It goes to show how easy it is. It's not about hours and hours of study. It's a change in perspective. I will let God handle this problem and here is what He says about loneliness; I choose to believe that, not my feelings.

Josie seemed to be adjusting all right since her mom's passing. I was glad she had Kenya to look forward to. She was spending a lot of time at our house as her dad was working on changing his second shift hours to first shift hours. We were glad to have her. She's a precious girl who has actually brought my two kids, Colton and Brooklyn closer together somehow.

DISTRACTIONS

It is easy to get distracted. There are many good projects that I want to help people with. I want to help in any way I can. One of my life-long struggles is the desire to help everyone. I learned that from my mom. For me, it led to some very damaging relationships in many ways… financially, emotionally, and even physically.

In December 2011, a long-time friend and spiritual mentor of mine had asked for my help on a project she was working on. I had prayed about it and God told me, help her get the legal part of this project started. So we worked together for a few weeks and had most of that part together. We enjoyed working together and she asked me to be a part of the Board. I immediately said "of course" not thinking anything of it because we had worked through so many details, and I have loved working with her.

We worked tirelessly day and night for months, generating ideas, fund raising, looking at properties, networking, and getting administrative details together for the organization. It entailed a lot of work including phone calls, paperwork, board meetings, mass mailings, and so on.

While we were in the middle of all our efforts, I had a planned trip to Israel with my mom and Fox River. Before leaving, my friend and I had a meeting, during which I explained where everything was at and what needed to be followed up on. Then I was on my way to Israel. While in Israel, God spoke to me and said He wanted me to back off the project. I assumed He meant just stop doing the busy work. Do my job as president of the Board but nothing else, and to let others pick up the other work. I was fine with that. So upon my return I was ready to say as much to my friend and the Board. But before I could do that, I got a phone call indicating that I was not handling things as they felt they should be handled, and if I wasn't going to change, then my services were no longer needed for the Board.

I was shocked. I had poured my heart and my soul into this organization for months. I didn't understand what specifically the problem or problems were we were even talking about. It was devastating to be treated this way by a spiritual ministry organization. I felt betrayed, slapped in the face, and so many other types of hurt, and I didn't understand what I did wrong.

This is a good example of spiritual warfare. When one goes on a trip that has a spiritual high associated with it… a mission trip, a trip to the Holy Land… the devil isn't happy. He doesn't want anyone to progress to a higher level, and he will hit in areas you are not expecting, with a blow that could sweep you off God's path into a downward spiral.

Though it wasn't easy, I took my pain and hurt to God about the situation. I did this by praying, journaling, and most of all by keeping my mouth shut. I wanted to talk about it to anyone and everyone who would listen to me. That would not have helped me get past those feelings. That would have left me stuck in them. I did speak of it with a few close spiritual friends, but that was all. I did not allow myself to talk about it very much. I could talk about it with God in prayer or journaling; I didn't need to talk with a person about it. That helped me get through the situation a lot quicker. I kept moving forward with God. Through prayer and journaling, God revealed to me that I had not prayed about taking on the position as president in this organization. I was asked and I took it. All the work I did was not work God had in mind for me. It was great and worthwhile work, it just wasn't where He wanted me.

It was brought to my consciousness that God wanted me working in Kenya and I spent so much time working on that organization that I was neglecting the work He wanted me to do for Kenya. It is difficult to raise funds here in the US for projects overseas. People and organizations like to focus on concerns within the US and even just in their local community. This other project was local, and it was going to be so much easier to generate support and funds that were needed. I had been burned out a little by lack of access to any funds to accomplish tasks in Kenya. So I had been distracted by this other, possibly easier, work.

As if on cue, right after this happened, I got an email from Vicky and Hellen outlining an event Hellen hosted with adoptive families.

I had not yet planned the trip for the spring I thought I would be taking. With all the work that I had been doing for this other organization, and the fact that I had just returned from a ten-day trip to Israel, I was going to put it off and just go in summer. This was the sign for me to book my spring trip, so I did that immediately. And thank God I did, because some major pieces fell into place on that trip.

5

MAY 2011

BACK ON FOCUS

This trip was very last minute. I think I booked the trip one month before I was going to be leaving. That is very unlike me. Generally I am a planner, and throwing something together without thinking through everything thoroughly, and having everything in place was not easy for me, but I knew it was what God wanted me to do.

When I arrived I was met by Kristen who was already in Kenya, and had been since the previous July. A fellow Kenyan traveler, Nora DeBoth joined us as well. Nora was going to Kenya for a month to student-teach and learn more about Kenyan schools and teaching. She was studying in Indiana at Anderson University that has a foreign 'student-teaching' program. She was not at that point in her schooling, but she wanted to see what it would be like. So she was to spend a month in Kenya in May 2011, and would be spending two weeks traveling around to various schools with Kristen and me, as well as two to three weeks in the Fox River Schools co-teaching.

NAIROBI – ADOPTION MEETINGS

We started the trip in Nairobi by visiting a few government officials.

The first day, my clothes didn't feel right, and I was tired.

I had a little 'fit' in the hotel room and then we were off. (I realize this was yet another sign that I needed to focus more on my health.)

We got a chance to meet the person in charge of adoptions and the full adoption process in Kenya, Judy Ndung'u. In September of 2009, the United States stopped issuing any visas for Kenyan children to come home to the US after being adopted due to some Hague Convention rules. Judy was in the process of writing new regulations for Kenyan adoption aimed to facilitate more international adoptions in compliance with The Hague Adoption Convention rules.

As a little side legal lesson, the Hague Convention was originally established in the early 1900s to provide an international court to address international concerns in an endeavor to avoid wars. On May 29, 1993, the Hague Adoption Convention was concluded at The Hague, in the Netherlands. This established international standards of practice for intercountry adoptions and other international child-related issues. One of the major reasons for the adoption section of the Hague Convention Treaty is to prevent child trafficking, which is a major problem in the United States and around the world. The United States signed the Adoption Convention in 1994, and the Convention was implemented in the United States in April 2008. Kenya has signed it as well, and it has been ratified by more than 80 other countries.

While adopting a child from a Convention country is similar in many ways to adopting a child from a country not party to the Convention, there are some key differences. In particular, those seeking to adopt receive greater protection if they adopt from a Convention country, as the processes are usually a bit more involved.

Anyway, Judy was great and she expressed gratitude that I didn't try and tell her what to do and how to do it, but instead went alongside her to see if there was anything I could do to facilitate the process, while listening to her ideas. I am so grateful I learned not to burn bridges early in the Kenyan research adoption process. At first I wanted to write a letter to the government and everyone else telling them their rules were not conducive to helping children; but I learned that this would hurt the process more than help it. am so glad I did not burn any bridges by sending a letter like that. I am also glad my great friend Erica showed me that is not how change happens. Coming alongside people and showing them love and compassion for our neighbor is how it happens.

For the rest of that day, I got a chance to visit three of the four accredited adoption agencies in Nairobi. We got the list from Judy, the adoption secretariat, and our driver Michael was amazing with directions and was able to get us to all three. We had time to talk with the agency's staff about international adoptions, their processes, and where they see problems in the process.

We went to Little Angels Network and talked to Caroline Macharia. At Kenya Children's Home we had a discussion with Susan. They had a little boy who was being adopted that day. At the Kenyans to Kenyans Peace Initiative (KKPI) we talked to Jackie.

At the time, KKPI was the agency that was able to get the process done the fastest, so I wanted to meet with their lawyer, Joram Mwenda, and talk to him. He was kind enough to let us go over right away. Joram was great and I learned a lot about the court process and workings of the adoption process from him.

There was one other accredited adoption agency in Kenya, but I was told by various sources that they were overwhelmed and not up to the best standard of work; so we did not meet there and would suggest working with one of the three agencies I did visit.

I was learning so much and meeting such great people.

IT'S A SMALL WORLD – AFTER ALL

Once we arrived in Mombasa, we visited a school in Ribe (just outside Mombasa on the east coast of Africa). There is quite a 'small world' story here. My friend Kristen was staying in Mombasa for one year when she went to this school and met a woman from Waukesha, Wisconsin who was working in the school for a year or so. Waukesha is where Kristen is from too. They then discovered that the chief of Ribe, has a brother who went to Carroll University in Waukesha, Wisconsin. Carroll University had sent books and shelving over for a library. The chief's brother, Allan, lives in South Milwaukee, Wisconsin which is 15 minutes from our home town. So we traveled around the world to meet a woman from Waukesha, and Tito, the chief of Ribe, whose brother is living 15 minutes from our house, and then help set up a library sent from a college ten minutes from our house that we had no knowledge of prior to walking into a classroom in the middle of nowhere at a school! Talk about small world.

After returning from that trip I was able to meet Allan and his family and say hello from Kenya in South Milwaukee. It's unbelievable how small this world really is.

The Ribe School had a fully stocked library sitting in boxes in a room in their school; but they had never been in a library so they had no idea how to organize a check-out system or set up the books. So we spent half a day, with the entire school helping, setting up the entire library and making check-out cards and systems for the kids to check out books.

It was great fun working alongside the kids and staff, and watching a room go from boxes of books, to a library that they can use. We left very simple written instructions for them on how the check out the process works and how it should be followed up on weekly.

Then there was yet another Kenyan/American reality check. In Kenya there is one library, in Nairobi, and unless you are a VIP, you cannot even check books out. I'm not even sure if you can get in the building. They have a few traveling libraries, but they don't come around often and I don't think you can even check out books from them. So access to books is very limited. That I cannot even fathom. We have a public library in EVERY small town, village, city in the United States; we have libraries in every school. So here in my town of less than 40,000 people, we have at least eight libraries, one in every elementary school, all the high schools and of course our public library. And these numbers don't even address the fact that I can go to my local library and ask them to search every library in the State and send me books from all of those libraries, all for free.

In Kenya, they don't even have access to one library. So it is no wonder this room sat with books in boxes and empty shelves. They have no concept about how a library looks or runs. They were left with instructions on how to set it up, but when you don't have any experience to base it on, how would you go about setting up a library? We have so many choices not available to others, yet we take it for granted every day. How can our realities be so different?

THE START OF PILGRIM'S ADOPTION RESOURCE CENTER (PARC)

After further prayer, steps, and discussions, God filled in the gaps that He wanted me to use my law degree, child care field, and UW-Whitewater undergraduate psychology degree to be able to reach out to the people and government of Kenya to facilitate and educate on adoptions. I learned some years later that at the same time (December 2009) God had put the same vision of making adoptions more prevalent and accepted in Kenya and supporting adoptive families on Hellen's heart.

With the continued realization that African culture does not even know what adoption is, God was continuing to lead. Even college-educated people think that orphanages are just places where you can go and spend time with parentless kids; but they do not know the children are available to take home and make part of their family after a surprisingly short legal process.

Adoption in Kenya had only started a short ten years ago, in 2001, with the ratifying of the Adoption Act.

Realizing this Vicky, Hellen, and I got to work. We met with adoptive parents to see where they felt the legal and social processes were breaking down to decide where we could best serve to fix the process. We made vision and mission statements and plans for the work that we felt needed to be done at this point. The focus was on setting up outlines on a variety of educational programs for police, lawyers, judges, teenagers, churches, and communities, to inform them about their roles in adoption, what adoption is, why it is important, and to dispel the rumors that adoption means 'buying babies'.

Hellen's main focus is on educating and counseling the public and potential adoptive families on how to handle issues that come up through adoption, as well as insecurity about their parenting skills and how to deal with community and school stigma.

My main focus was an outreach for pregnant woman, to let them know that there are options for them. Abortion is illegal in Kenya, though it is occurring and it is not pretty. I've heard disturbing stories of women drinking bleach because they believe that it will kill the baby. Instead it kills the mother! I have also heard many other horror stories that are even worse than this for both moms and babies. Also, abandoning babies in pit latrines or on the side of the road is all too common in Kenya. While I have been there on trips, various news stories have arisen with people finding babies in pit latrines, babies left on the side of the road being mauled by dogs, and those are the ones you hear about. I don't want to think about the number of babies who are never found, and simply left cold and alone to die. There are safe haven laws in Kenya, and new mothers can drop their babies off at various places, no questions asked; but they are not aware of these laws. Education is the key to change.

We had also discussed opening a much needed adoption agency, strictly based in Mombasa, to handle adoptions for all the coastal orphanages that want the necessary services. The idea was that there would be a lawyer and a psychologist under the same roof, to get the process completed a lot faster and without the frustrating delays seen in the experience of others. The other factor was to be able to help clients with their paperwork process, which can be overwhelming. Adoption isn't cheap, so finances are already a stress, and then to be dropped a knee-deep packet of paperwork is very overwhelming for most people, especially when they are already stressed. We wanted to be able to be alongside to help people through the process. In addition we wanted to start a scholarship fund for domestic and international adoptions. This would be a fund where people could donate to help offset the costs of adoption for a family that would love, and be able to afford, another child, but could not afford the cost of adoption itself. A general figure for a domestic adoption in Kenya in 2012 was around US$500-700. That is a lot of money in Kenya. But if we could set up scholarships for eligible families, that would go a long way towards helping these children find good loving homes.

We also did preliminary budgets. We did budgets based on purchasing a building and budgets based on renting office space. We began working on getting funding to host the educational programs, and begin other work. Once the work had started, to get to the next level, we needed more substantial funds, but one step at a time.

Most of these efforts were intended to help with domestic adoptions. But in my heart I also wanted to see international adoptions expanded. If we can get good homes for some Kenyan children outside of Kenya, that will leave Kenyan children, in Kenya, with a better standard of living. It could help alleviate some of the pressure on the government and its agencies. To that end, I was meeting with various Kenyan government officials and lawyers in Nairobi who are involved in the adoption process. I was learning more from them about the process and where it was at and going to, and developing relationships.

The scariest thing I walked away from Kenya hearing this time was that the orphanages at the coast, do not conduct any legal adoptions. I was told that there were simply no regulations and that the purpose of these institutions is primarily to get large donations from the UK and the US. I have to believe that if this is true, they would not be opposed to selling a child if the donations were not forthcoming. Worse still, selling a child would most likely involve a child being sold into child slavery of some type.

Now I was beginning to see why God put me through law school. I had been beginning to think the US$170,000 student loan bill was a waste of time and money (as I was, by then, running a home child care center); but God has His way of bringing things around.

SCHOOL PRESENTATIONS

While we were in Ribe at the schools, we got a chance to talk to high school girls. All three of us, Nora, Kristen and I, asked the girls what they wanted to do when they grew up, and gave suggestions on how to stick with their goals, even when it was hard. We also discussed with them how pregnancy would interfere with those goals and informed them about the option of adoption if they had friends or family in a situation. It was the first, unofficial Pilgrim's Adoption Resource Center (PARC) presentation!

We also spent some time at schools on the south coast doing educational programs. We discussed their dreams and goals, and how to keep focused on these goals. We also talked to girls about how to reach out to avoid early marriages (11, 12 13-year-old girls are being sold into marriage and/or prostitution by their parents because of poverty); how to avoid pregnancy; adoption and what it is; and other topics. These are tough topics for little girls to deal with, but this is their reality. It made me think of my daughter at home, this same age, but facing a totally different reality.

Our program with the police, and my discussions with people in Nairobi were intended to find out more about this situation so we could address any necessary issues. We were hoping these programs would begin running as early as June 2011, assuming we could get funds rolling.

JUDGMENT IS DIFFICULT

The more I am out there asking people for help on Facebook, and other ways, both financially and through time donations, I am increasingly in a position to be judged. It is very hard to raise funds and work for kids around the world. I face comments in the States like, "There are kids here that need help." And I do not disagree with that statement.

It is sometimes a struggle to keep going. Remember, I never had a desire to travel the world. This is something God placed for me, not something I chose. And hearing comments like that can pull the winds out of your sails at times. But I have come to realize that individuals who make those types of comments are usually doing little or nothing to help people here or anywhere else in the world. They are quick to pass judgment on what others are doing, but are slow to do anything to help in any way. It is not easy raising funds for projects around the world. A lot of help is needed and funding sources can be far and few between for any international work. The claim that we only help in the local community is something I read and hear a lot. That can be hard to handle and very discouraging.

One part of both of these issues for me now is that we in the United States do not understand what life is like in most of the world. We don't have any inkling that even the most desperate people here have it so much better than almost everyone in Kenya and two-thirds of the world. They live on less than US$1 per day. They don't have food pantries, food stamps, health care, college loans, or anyone around to help them. We have some built-in protections against those things in our country. We have so much to be grateful for that we don't even realize. That being said, not everyone is called to work in Kenya. Some are called to work right here in the US. And in fact, we are all called to 'work' every day of our lives wherever we are. Right here at home, with our own children and neighbors, in our cities, around our States, and around the world. Every day should be a mission trip.

So let's all pull together, and whatever God is calling us to do, let's get out there and do it. Let's stop making excuses that we are too busy, or that we will do it when our kids are older, or when this happens or that happens. We need to clear a little bit of time out of schedules; cut out one extra-curricular activity to allow time; do it while we are waiting for someone to finish their activity; turn off the TV or computer for a few minutes every day; or find projects we can work on with our kids. And we need to do it. Let's put all those excuses aside and just do something today, as little as it may be, to step forward with God and make a difference. That may be spending more time with Him to figure out what it is that He wants us to do, or maybe it is doing it. Whatever it is for you, spend some time today doing it. You will be glad you did.

As for me, I was destined to return to Kenya in a few short months to continue this journey with two amazing 13-year-old girls who have a whole lifetime ahead of them to change the world.

Brooklyn (right) and Josie seen presenting a Bible study lesson on letting your "light" overcome the darkness.

SCRAPBOOK ALBUM

KENYA 2008–2012

Carrie, giving hope to the kids in Kenya.

The ten-year-old girl from Vipingo with her brother on her back.

A simple pen to Kenyan kids is more valuable that the latest PlayStation game is to American kids.

Kristen Pettigrew, a US neighbor that Carrie flew around the world to meet in Kenya in 2008.

Life in Kenya. A young girl carrying around her siblings.

Pat Molitor, another neighbor Carrie met in Kenya during 2008.

A working woman carrying brooms on her head on the way to market.

Carrie and her son Colton on safari in Kenya during July 2008.

The harsh reality of life in Kenya; babies taking care of babies.

KENYAN SCHOOLS

Children at school examine a colorful parachute.

This was the exact moment in Bomani when Carrie was reminded of her high school dream to work with children in child care.

This is the only meal these children in Vipingo, Kenya will get today. They will not get any food at home.

83

2009: Carrie surrounded by some of the Kenyan kids she has got to love.

2008: Colton teaching the children at Bomani basketball for the first time.

Each of the kids has a story, many of which are heartbreaking.

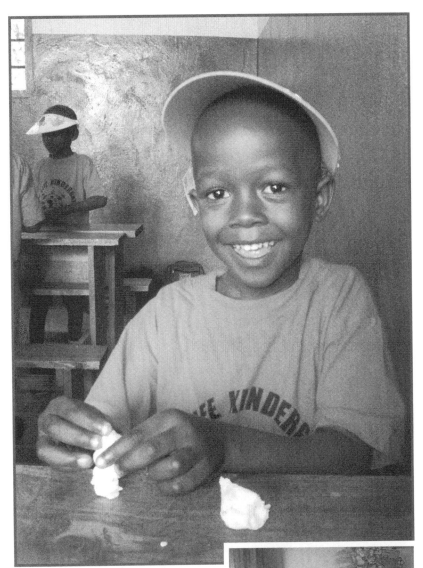

2009: Alfred with playdough during a Bible lesson focusing on building people up.

Left: A 2009 KG-1 class making name-tag visors.

Money for educational resources in Kenya is tight, so kids dont often get the luxury of 'free' drawing.

Kids painting with watercolors for the first time in their lives.

Conditions in free Kenyan schools are less than ideal, often with one teacher to 100 kids. Many children are forced to sit on the floor and share books.

The conditions in our church schools are completely different: proper desks, smaller class sizes, every child has his or her own books.

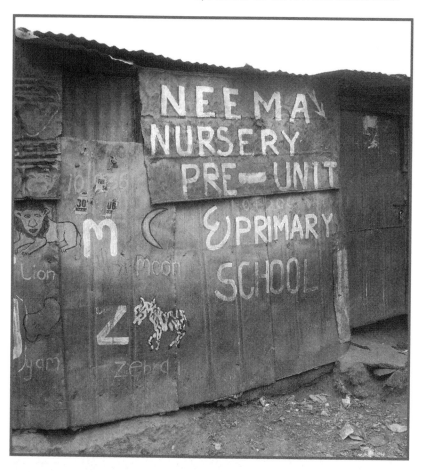

Below: Bentas schoolroom in Kinera for HIV-positive children

A free school in Kibera.

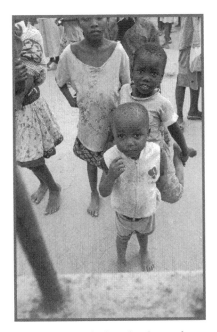 

Children outside the school gates have little hope.

Happiness for Kibera kids is to be able to get into school.

Kids in a school in Kibera are forced to make the best of what they have got.

89

Carrie with some of the kids during recess at Bomani.

Left: Carrie shares English books with kids at the school.

Below: Carrie with kids during recess at Vipingo.

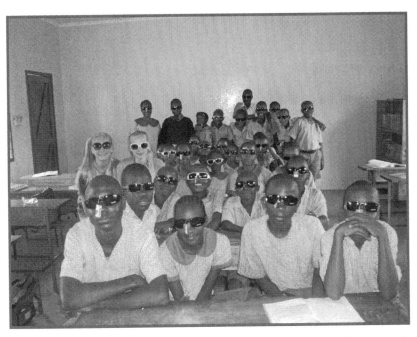

Sunglasses for Tiwi (some still with their labels on): Let your light shine so bright you need sunglasses!

Brooklyn and Josie play with kids during a recess at Vipingo.

Brooklyn with Diana, a little girl who didn't want to leave her side.

Chris on his crutches while on Safari in Kenya during 2009.

While mountain climbing Carrie found she had to use 'everything' and was still struggling to get to the top.

Brooklyn and Kristen enjoy the beautiful view on top of the mountain.

Edgar and Michael, grateful for a small cup of porridge for breakfast.

Carrie presenting on 'stranger danger' at a school in Tiwi.

Carrie with Marian and Alfred at Bomani during July 2010.

Luann DeBoth and an older student at Tiwi.

Chris participating in tug-o-war during 2009, even though he had a broken leg.

93

The mud hut-making team hard at work.

When the team started the mud hut project, the family was excited, but the man was hesitant. But by the time it was complete, even he was smiling.

94

Community Outreach Days

When you get off the bus on Community Outreach Day, the crowd is so big, it's like being a movie star.

Colton playing basketball with some of the young men of Kenya on a Community Outreach Day.

In Bomani, everyone packs into the church hall on Community Outreach Day.

Community Outreach Day has been a great success right from the start. Just look at this crowd. This is a small idea of how many people show up time after time.

Kids on Outreach Day looking for gum wrappers to write on.

Carrie with the ten-year-old girl in Vipingo who could not write.

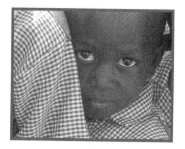

Brooklyn using some of her talents during a Community Outreach Day.

Josie and Brooklyn with some of the kids who came for the day.

Brooklyn holds a child in need.

Left: Behind every little face there is a story, usually sad.

Right: Brooklyn, Josie and Carrie hanging out at Bomani with the community on one of the successful Community Outreach Days they helped to organize.

MWANAROSE

Right: Mwanarose seen with Carrie in October 2010.

Mwanarose, cute and confident, in 2009.

Mwanarose with Carrie in Kenya during 2009.

Mwanarose (right) with her school friend Victoria in 2010.

Mwanarose photographed during 2011.

Mwanarose with her family; all brothers.

FOOD GLORIOUS FOOD

Kids in Bomani eating lunch.

For most of the children, this is their only meal of the day.

Standing in line, waiting for food on Outreach Day.

This is the kind of meal these children can expect when they come to school. Most get nothing to eat at home.

WATER FOR SURVIVAL

A village is using filty, dirty swamp water for drinking and for cooking. It's all they have got.

Brooklyn and Josie, baptised in the Indian Ocean in July 2011.

Young kids seen getting water. This is their future, even though the girl in the front is clearly old enough to be in school. Only a few lucky ones get there.

NEW FRIENDS & FAMILY

Relationships take on a whole new meaning in Kenya. While Brooklyn and these Kenyan kids had never met, and in fact don't even understand what the other person says (in terms of language), they 'understand' each other perfectly.

Since becoming involved in Community Outreach Days, we now have local friends who join us. This is Penninah hanging out with some of my favorite friends at Bomani - Mariam and Alfred and a few others.

Kids running after the bus as fast as they can, for as long as they can.

101

Kids on the wall. It is still a desperate situation for the kids outside the school. They wait, hoping they will be amongst the next batch to get the opportunity to improve their lives, or at least get a glimpse of the hope of others.

Above: Carrie helps Henzie put on his new clothes; something he never believed would happen.

Left: Henzie arrives in his tattered clothes.

THE STREETS & VILLAGES OF KENYA

Buildings in Kibera... if you can call them that! For the rest it is wet and filthy.

Above & Below: Street markets are commonplace in Kenyan towns and cities.

Arched elephant tusks are a constant reminder that this is Africa.

Above: Filth in the streets of Kibera.

Left: Rotting rubbish lies upstream to the water that runs alongside the homes in this town.

A picturesque village belies the truth of how people really live.

Most villagers live in "quaint" huts made of mud and corrugated iron.

This is how most of the people live in the villages. It's all they have.

ORPHANS & ORPHANAGES

During Carrie's visit in March 2012, they used books that had been written and illustrated especially for them.

Left: Carrie and a baby from the Good Life Orphanage.

Below Left: Helen, Carrie and Vicky at the kick-off for the Pilgrims Adoption Resource Cnter,

Below: An orphan in a a baby swing.

Good Life Orphanage provides what many children would consider luxuries in life.

Clothes are regularly contributed to the Good Life Orphanage, for the children.

Tiny, wee orphans... unable to help themselves. These babies were being cared for at the Upende Orphanage in Kenya.

SOME OF THE PEOPLE WHO CARE

Pastor Allan and Eve his wife are amazing people who have made much of this missionary work possible.

Pastor Paul from Vipingo who helps us so much.

Jim and Susie Horne, missionaries to Kenya for more than 30 years, created Operation Give Hope and sit on the Board of Directors.

And there we were, walking the streeets! From left to right: Carrie, Maureen, Sue Paul's aunt and Rose.

Baby Life Rescue: Peter with his adopted children

Liz with Carrie, all set to take photos of all those involved with the Community Outreach Days.

Right: Carrie discusses adoption issues with Grace from Little Angels Adoption Network

110

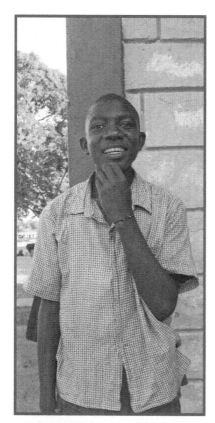

Above: An awesome hand-painted wall inside the church at Vinpingo is a reminder of God's love.

Left: Teddy, an amazing teenager from Vipingo who helps Carrie and her team so much.

Brooklyn and Carrie experienced moments of tears and moments of great joy while in Kenya together.

6

PARENTING, UGH

For this trip, I had the company of both my daughter, Brooklyn, and her friend, Josie. The outbound flights were very difficult for me this time, which is unusual. The rule is to sleep on all flights to get your rest. It takes two days with eight hours time change to get there, which usually means two days of sleeping on an airplane and being ready to roll when you arrive on the third morning. I have never had a problem with that, but, for some reason, I could not get to sleep on this trip. I tried everything I could and nothing worked. In one of my efforts, I watched a movie, which usually does the trick.

The movie dealt with the death of a mom, so it made me sad and nervous for Josie. What if, after the trip, the events of the past year, hit her hard and the reality of her mom's death were to throw her into a tailspin? Would I know what to do? Would I be there to help her? Would she be okay? Brooklyn, my daughter had lost her dad too. Would she be okay? I couldn't stop crying.

Then God started bringing up issues from my past that He wanted me to address. I kept telling Him that I had dealt with them and that there was nothing more. But in this moment of complete breakdown, in the middle of an airplane, it was obvious there was more to deal with. Luckily most of the people on the plane were sleeping. God was speaking volumes to me and all

I had available to write on without waking up the girls was the air sickness bag. So I listed all the things God was showing me: reach out to the ministry that had pushed me away earlier in the year; write about things I have gone through in life and things I would rather not think about let alone write about; and on and on.

I took a deep breath and made a note of all those things on the bag for further reference when I got home.

FACING CHALLENGES

It was a lot of work preparing the girls, and a lot of work getting the money together, and a **lot** of mental energy for me to live in one room with two teenagers for almost three weeks; but God did wonderful things through it for both me and the girls.

Probably because of the cost and the amount of work that we had all put into this trip in time and money, I had a lot of expectations, for myself, for Brooklyn and probably even Josie; and mostly, if I was truthful, when it comes down to it, of God.

I wanted this to be the perfect trip for Josie and I wanted her to experience everything Brooklyn and I had. I really did want it to be perfect. I had to learn and practice a lot of letting go and letting God handle things instead of me trying to control them.

Over my lifetime, attempting to control situations that were beyond my control has been a reccurring issue. It has led to bad relationships and even worse, staying in bad relationships. This usually happens because I have unrealistic expectations of both myself and others.

Al-Anon and the Center for Creative Learning really helped me start on this journey of letting go of controlling other people and focusing on controlling my own thoughts about situations. I was learning to not hold on too tightly to ideas or expectations of what I think things should be or how things should go, but instead expect (hope for the best) and then see (what ends up happening and deal with it then, not in advance).

So instead of EXPECTANCY we should EXPECT AND SEE. In the end, it is God who helped me to let go of all people and situations in my life. And it is an ever-continuing process. As is probably evident, reading this book, anxiety is a reccurring thing for me. I become anxious when things are not exactly as I expect and/or want them to be.

There were times in my life when, if plans changed at the last minute, I would go crazy. For example, planning something as simple as going to go to the park and then deciding we were going to the museum instead. In my head, I had planned out what we needed for the park, the time it would take at the park, and how I would fit everything else I needed to fit into the day around going to the park. If someone would try to change that at the last minute, I couldn't handle it. That is just one simple example, so you can probably imagine how larger things would throw me off even more.

Through prayer and reading the Bible, I am now able to have peace, even if plans change, even if I cannot get everything done in a day that I want to. I can turn that situation over to God and have peace in the moment. And on the bigger situations, my kids and relationships, God has shown Himself faithful to handle those too so I don't have to worry about them. He's got it taken care of, and even if He didn't, which I know He does, I cannot do anything productive or helpful about them by worrying so what's the point? It just wastes time and energy on things that will never matter.

I would much rather focus that time and energy on my relationship with God and others than worrying.

You have to think of worry as a trade off. You have the option to worry if that is what you would like, but you also have the option of letting it go.

Choosing worry does nothing to further you or anyone else

forward; it keeps you stuck in the past and usually extremely frustrated. Choosing to focus on something else while God takes care of your worrisome situation can lead to peace and productive use of your time and energy.

Parenting is always a challenge for me. Trying to find the balance between teaching, controlling, yelling, and anything else, including where I end and where God takes over, and how that changes at the different ages of the kids is a constant struggle for me. It has become especially difficult during the teenage years of my children, when the start of letting go is natural, yet I don't like it, especially where the line isn't clear.

As you can probably imagine, this trip presented some parenting challenges, especially living in the same room with teenagers and having nowhere to go to be alone. It led to a few tears even. My Kenyan bathroom 'mirror moments' on this trip entailed things like, "Really, God? This is more than I could or should have to deal with. She thinks she knows everything. She is so messy; stuff is everywhere. She doesn't listen to anything I have to say. She doesn't stop talking… and why is she so disrespectful? Why doesn't she just trust me and learn from my mistakes? Help me deal with her; I don't know what to do with her".

And then I had a moment, after I finally stopped talking. I noticed that exactly what I was complaining about to God regarding my daughter was exactly what I was doing. Thoughts started swimming in my head: "That is how people have related to me their whole lives, Carrie, just like a teenager." What? I think I know more than God. I don't listen. I don't trust God. I think I know it all. I don't stop talking. I don't learn from the mistakes of others. Then I realized it was true.

We control situations. If I do this and this, this will happen. We jump in ahead of God instead of praying for guidance. Maybe we even pray for guidance but then we decide decisions need to be made quicker than answers are coming so we just move forward. And I do rarely stop talking.

Oh my gosh... to God I am a teenager!

TEENS EXPERIENCE THE TRIP

During our year-long prep time, the girls wrote a Bible study assignment and some other presentations to share with the Tiwi academy on the south coast. The Bible study process was about being the Light of the world and overtaking the darkness. They wrote it themselves and presented it very well.

Then we gave sunglasses to everyone at the school to remind them that they should shine so 'light' that people need 'shades'. The glasses were new to them and they were grateful. To get a gift like this... something as simple as sunglasses, is like Christmas morning to them. Most of the kids were shocked to even be able to try them on, let alone get to keep them.

I offer special thanks to family and friends who helped pay for the 350 pairs of sunglasses we needed to bring, one for every student and staff on the grounds. We also spent some time learning a lot about their school system and what they want to be when they grow up... and we shared the same with them.

Back at Bomani, a few days later, Josie fell in love with a little boy named Nevy at the Bomani School. He is adorable. Brooklyn had the cutest little girl from Bomani, Diana, following her around. When it came time for lunch, Brooklyn knelt down and said to Diana, "Wait here, I'll be back soon." Then she moved towards the dining hall to go and eat. She wasn't ten steps away, and heading toward the dining hall, when Diana came running and grabbed her hand as if to say, "Don't leave me here alone". Needless to say, she joined us, and ate with us.

The girls were baptized in the Indian Ocean while we were there. One of the lessons we had before going to Kenya was on Believer's Baptism and that baptism is one way we show God that we love Him and want to follow His ways. I didn't want to influence their decision, thinking that they had to do it as part of our class. So I just presented it, saying it was possible to be baptized in Kenya and to let me or Pastor Guy or Denise know by the beginning of the trip if they wanted to do it. They both immediately, and without hesitation said they would like to be baptized while they were in Kenya. Big thanks to God for their hearts. So one rather chilly morning we waded into the Indian Ocean with most of the group and Pastor Guy baptized them.

When I asked them what their biggest take-away was from the trip, I heard things I was not expecting to hear. Brooklyn indicated that the 'smells' had affected her most. Mombasa, specifically, has a certain smell. I couldn't put my finger on it at first, until I smelled the same thing here in the States one day driving around. I stopped and said to myself, "It smells like Kenya, what is that?" It was burning garbage. There are piles of garbage on the sides of the road all the time and it is lit afire, a lot releasing a distinct odor into the air.

Josie said that her take-away was watching the people on the streets and how close they get to the cars, and how handicapped (especially blind and wheelchair-bound) people are in the middle of the streets begging for money from the cars. She saw one man fall out of his wheelchair onto the street and was very concerned about him. That stayed in her mind for more than a year.

Since Josie had never been on such a trip, I think she truly enjoyed spending time with the kids. Both she and Brooklyn realized how much they had to be grateful for at home, and they returned motivated to do better in school so they could be the best they could be, and share that with the rest of the world... wherever that might be in the future. Both would like to go to

117

Kenya again, but probably on a medical mission-type trip as they would both like to go into the medical field.

Since they're only in the eighth grade, this could change. They both learned a lot and saw a lot, and hopefully will make different choices than I made with money and life decisions as they get older. Brooklyn found this trip to be a little boring as it was the same schedule as the previous year.

God also took some time to show me the other side. It was good to see some of the qualities in Brooklyn that drive me nuts trying to parent, being put to good use through teaching and interacting with a lot of kids. Brooklyn and Josie were both like the pied piper walking around the Vipingo fun day with 100s of kids following them around. They would play Simon-says-type games and then they taught them English and other fun things. I smiled as I reflected that the non-stop loud-talking mouth being put to great use producing a day these kids will never forget. I also thought back to London and how Brooklyn was able to help us navigate the London Underground as well as their other subway systems, without pause. This being an example of the good head on her shoulders, and how she uses it well a lot of times.

These situations gave me pause to think how God reacts more this way to our faults than the way I was reacting to the qualities earlier. He looks and focuses on how our qualities are put to good use, not on ways in which we mess up sometimes. That's the key to parenting I guess.

PILGRIM'S ADOPTION RESOURCE CENTER UPDATE

I got a few chances early in the trip to meet with my adoption partners, Vicky and Hellen. We opened a bank account, finished up the budgets, made a decision on a logo, and set up our first meeting with a community group to start the education process about domestic adoption.

They hosted the meeting in August 2011 shortly after I left, and it went well.

WORK AT HOME

Upon returning home, I continued the work I had started during the previous fall, getting an office and promotional materials for Operation Give Hope up and running. Pat Molitor and I were meeting weekly for a year drafting letters, going through thousands of photos, creating brochures, compiling church databases, brainstorming, organizing, and creating presentations.

In my search for partners to work on fund raising, I searched for groups on college campuses in the Milwaukee area that had 'Africa clubs.' As I mentioned before, it is difficult to find people who are interested in working for causes that are not local and I thought this would be a great fit. I went online and found a few of these clubs at local universities and colleges and contacted them via email. There was only one that contacted me back, but that was all that was needed.

A lovely woman, Adelina Alphonce, from Alverno College, a local women's college in the Milwaukee area responded. Adelina is from Tanzania and was listed as the president of the Friends of Africa Club for Alverno online. She was at Alverno with two or three other women from Kenya. We set up a time in late June for me to bring the girls down and say hello as part of one of our weekly meetings before we left on our July 2011 trip. We met and exchanged a few follow-up emails indicating that nothing happens on campus during the summer; so we knew she would be in contact in the fall.

I was so involved with getting back from Kenya and finding funding sources and other things, that I didn't think much about the Alverno contact. Then, in the fall, I had two contacts from people I did not know at Alverno. One was a girl in charge of the Friends of Africa Club that year. We met and talked about doing a few fund raisers, though with busy college students who are working and going to school, it was not the right timing for those events.

The other contact came from a professor at the Alverno Business School. His name was Robert Birney and he teaching a business class where he contacts various nonprofit and other organizations to get lists of available needs in the area. In the class, teams are formed and then they pick what group they would like to work with given the tasks for that organization. The groups have to choose a cause, and work with that organization to bring it to the next level, depending on the organization's needs and the strengths of the students in that group. Happily, Adelina Alphonce remembered me and suggested he use Operation Give Hope as one of the organizations.

So that fall semester I was privileged to be able to work with Jenniffer Kerlin and Cherie Samolinski. They did a lot of research for Operation Give Hope on how to best approach people for sponsorships by researching how other organizations do it, and the best option for us to use to be able to take credit cards for child sponsorships. They also reviewed our current letters and brochures and made suggestions for improvements and started a Power Point presentation suggesting we approach area churches and other groups to do speaking engagements.

Within a week of receiving the report, Operation Give Hope had credit card acceptance available on our website for child sponsorships and it was being used. They also did some market research on whether they thought it would be acceptable to move from US$20 per month sponsorship amount to US$25 per month sponsorships to cover rising food and labor costs as well as some administrative costs of taking credit cards.

This was fantastic. A lot of work was being accomplished and I didn't have to do all the leg work. I just had to do the final few steps.

In the winter semester, Operation Give Hope was teamed up with Carrie Prince, Elyse Kohlbeck, and Denise Luke. These girls took a different approach. It was a much more get-out-there-in-front-of-people marketing and getting the word out approach. They worked with some local morning TV shows, and they got me some face-time with some large area churches. It lead to quite a few sponsorships and spreading the word of Operation Give Hope and the work being done.

I had a wonderful time speaking to, and talking with, the people of St. Augustine Catholic Church in Bay View, Wisconsin in March, 2012. Stephanie Gregory has wonderful spunk and personality and a passion to help people. Also, the Alverno girls suggested selling scarves to raise funds as well.

This is where the idea for this book started.

After the presentation I did for the church, a few people came up and asked me if I had a book, and I told them I didn't and had never even thought of writing one.

Alverno College is consistently listed as one of the top mid-west colleges in national magazines and I can see why. Volunteering is a very important part of the educational process at Alverno. They have a thermometer in the main building showing how many volunteer hours the students had booked that year, with the goal being set high. Alverno is a college that is changing the world. I'm proud to be working so closely with them. They are making a huge impact in Milwaukee and around the world.

For the rest of 2011 until March 2012, I would stay in the States working on funding sources and a lot of other administrative things (including websites and Facebook). I began sending most of the money I would have spent to travel, to my partners, to pay for expenses for the PARC. I was also looking into new funding sources.

My brother has worked in politics for much of his life in one way or another. After some discussions with him, I contacted Russ Feingold, a former Wisconsin congressman who did a lot of work for Africa in the Congress. In fact, when Russ left Congress, there were various articles in Kenyan and other African national papers stating what a loss it was going to be for Africa that he was no longer in Congress. He had also recently started teaching at Marquette University Law School, the school I had graduated from. I learned so much there and the staff and education was top-notch.

He led me to a woman who worked on his staff, who gave me some great places to contact for funding sources. I also looked into Rule of Law Institute (ROLI), Joyce Meyer Ministries, area churches, and Wisconsin Foundations. A lot of these larger organizations want a track record of your work and won't fund anything until you can show five or more years of work with measurable results. At the time of writing, nothing large had come to pass. It was a constant internal struggle. But as I continued to pray and ask, I couldn't wait to see what God would do.

A few years ago I meet Ken Kernen. He was a friend of a friend, and our mutual friend was living in Kenya. So she asked us to meet to discuss Ken possibly going on a trip to Kenya. Over the past few years, Ken and I had been planning a trip. We ramped up our efforts at this point, and were heavily planning our activities for a June 2012 trip. It was wonderful to work with someone who shares the passion for Kenya, and he hadn't even been there yet. I cannot wait to see what God does in his life and the life of his church, Risen Savior Lutheran Church in Franklin, Wisconsin.

Also during this time, I renewed my connection with the church I had grown up in, Hales Corners Lutheran. God works in mysterious ways, by now I know this. Colton was struggling with a certain class or two at our public school in New Berlin. After going through various testing procedures and meeting with various doctors, psychologists, and eventually an amazing neuropsychologist, Robert Newby, we were referred to Milwaukee Lutheran High School in Wauwatosa, Wisconsin 30 minutes from our home.

All this transpired and came to a head at the end of June 2011. I had obviously not planned on private high school tuition, which runs a person around US$9,000, so I was looking into every financial aid options I had available to us. One such option was a scholarship open to members of certain churches. It just so happened that the church I was confirmed in (and therefore was a member of), Hales Corners Lutheran, fitted the bill. The staff at Milwaukee Lutheran encouraged me to reach out to Hales Corners and reconnect to see if they would help. I was not overly excited about the fact at the time, but now I know how much God has used that church to change me even more.

With the school contract, we had to commit to attending their church regularly. After some discussion it was decided that I would attend at least every other weekend as I still wanted to remain at Fox River. As I started going, I realized how much I enjoyed the church. I got involved with the women's Bible study on Monday evenings. It was a really great experience. The church was very welcoming and had great sermons.

Hales Corners is a very mission-oriented church both locally and internationally. They do great work all around the world. I am so lucky to be a part of such a great community.

Milwaukee Lutheran has been an amazing school for Colton. They have helped so much with the areas he struggles in with school. But, because Colton is going to school over 30 minutes one-way, and there is no bus for him, it has been a lot more difficult to travel to Kenya during this time period.

But soon God put someone in my path who lead me to the exact time and place to book my next ticket.

7

GETTING THERE IS HALF THE BATTLE, I HOPE

It was Friday, the day we were leaving once again for Kenya. I had been fighting sickness since the previous Monday night – throat, headache, sinuses, cough, chest pains when coughing, and then stomach troubles on top of that. I went to the doctor at 2.15 pm and we were scheduled to leave at 5 pm. I hadn't slept in over a day and was so emotionally shot over being sick, coupled with the lack of sleep, I burst into tears at the doctor's office, simply because he told me I had a 101.2 degree temperature… even though I felt cold then at times during the day felt as if I had been burning up, which must have been due to an enormously high fever.

The doctor at the Pro Health Care was very understanding, supportive, and helpful. He gave me a short dose of fast-acting antibiotics for my sinuses and listened to my lungs a few times to make sure there wasn't any sign of pneumonia. He encouraged me to follow-up once I got to Kenya if I didn't feel any better.

I haven't mentioned the fact that at this point in time, my kids weren't responding to my messages. So I couldn't say goodbye and be sure that someone knew exactly where they were and where they intended to be for the night. Needless to say this was not what I had planned when I booked this trip at the beginning of January.

125

My friend, Sue Huerta, who was accompanying me on this trip was also sick, although not quite as severely.

So there I was, a little over one hour before leaving, sitting in my kitchen crying. This was not how it was supposed to be. I was sick. I was tired. My kids seemed to have fallen off the planet. I hadn't eaten anything but half a bowl of Romaine noodles and Wendy's fries since the previous Tuesday, and now I was suppose to eat a full meal, which I would have to cook myself, even though I couldn't even stand due to weakness and fatigue. I also needed to take six pills, which, remember, I could not swallow without ice cream. Having a rotten stomach, ice cream doesn't sound at all good. I ate the noodles and took the pills. I felt no better but it was time to go. After emptying half of my carry-on items, as I knew I was too weak to carry them, my husband, Chris and I headed out the door.

Even though I saw it as being very tough at the time, God was at work in this situation all along. First of all, I thanked God that Chris and I asked our friend Darrell to come with us to Chicago, to the airport, which we had never done before. Now I know why. I couldn't even attempt to pick up a bag other than my carry-on without getting extremely dizzy and almost passing out. I was also grateful that Sue was going with me. I had traveled to Kenya by myself the last few times, or was with teens; so to have an adult there, given my condition, was a relief.

As it turned out, once we were inside the airport loop at O'Hare, I began to feel much better. My strength was returning, I was able to speak without crying at every turn. Chris and Darrell helped us with all the baggage. We had enough donations to cover the extra baggage fees, for two extra bags, which totalled US$420.

It taught me a huge lesson about God's timing. Though I would have preferred to have been fully functional and healthy, God knew I wouldn't be, so He provided the help I needed to get to where I needed to be at the time. He needed me to be in Kenya and He provided Darrell, Sue and Chris to help with that. It's a lesson I need to learn over and over again, but I think I am finally seeing it *before* situations rather than having to wait till after to see it like I used to do.

ORPHANAGE VISITS

I didn't know Sue well prior to this trip. We had met briefly on the Fox River mission trip the summer before. Other than riding on the bus next to her once for a short time, and praying during that time, we had no other contact with one other.

Sue indicated she might be interested in going to Kenya with me. I was very surprised but excited. We both decided to pray about it, and a week later we booked the tickets to Kenya for a few months later. They were the least expensive tickets I have ever booked… less than US$1,000 each.

Once our travel was booked, we had to decide what we were meant to do when we got there. We prayed about where God was leading us. Sue indicated that she felt led to visit orphanages in Kenya. It made a lot of sense because Sue runs a group day care center in Wind Lake, Wisconsin, called 'Little VIPs' and I run a day care facility out of my home.

We decided on an art project with the kids using their fingerprints. I planned to take some pictures back home and frame them with photographs of the children, and their stories and art work, and sell these to help further the mission work.

Then we had a children's book written by Erica Brobrofsky, a friend of mine, and illustrated by Sara Treptow, a friend of Sue's. It's a wonderful book that tells about the fall of man into sin, and Jesus coming to save us if we choose Him, and then the Holy Spirit coming to help us through life. Sue would read the story to the kids and I would follow up with questions about the story and how it applies to their lives.

The kids know so much and are easy to talk to. We would then talk with them about how they have a purpose in their lives for being right where they are, and how they need to pray and read the Bible and ask God what His purpose is for them, just as Sue and I did. Like our decision is what brought us to them, God has a purpose for each child, and they needed to seek Him to find it. We left gifts of Bibles, flour, pens, and other office supplies for them.

While we had been busy planning the activities, Pastor Paul from Vipingo was setting up orphanages for us to visit. First we went to Shanzu Orphans Home, a place nearby. There we met a wonderful German woman who manages this orphanage. It was clean and well organized and the kids were great. The place was close enough to the ocean, so one could walk to the beach; some of the kids were already headed there when we arrived.

The German woman travels back and forth from Germany to Kenya to obtain funding for the center. She was in the middle of adding a second story to her building so she can house more children, but the project costs keep increasing. She had a million Kenyan schillings raised, but by then needed 1.6 million to finish the project. They have a very nice visitor suite if one wants to stay and play with the kids for as long as desired.

Baraka Academy is located way out in the middle of the bush, amidst rolling hills and valleys, at a place one can see the ocean from a far distance, in the village of Mwakiunge.

Once we arrived, we met with the young house moms first, and they showed us around the place. The boys' dorm is separated very far from the girls' dorm. The space is tight, but full of love. They have a hard time getting funds for food for the children, but they have education sponsors for all of them. I decided that I would like to help them get the cheapest food available, and maybe get food from an aid organization for all the great work they are doing: they take in abused and neglected cases from the Department of Children.

The director met with us. She had excellent organization for each child. All paperwork was completed and neatly in its place. It was interesting to see the internal workings of the center – all the files and administrative details. She indicated that some of her children get adopted after doing what she called international fostering. An Italian family petitioned the court for one year with one of the children in Italy.

For 90 days the director went with the child to Italy for a bonding period. Then the court approved the child to live there for a year alone. One year later, they petitioned the court again and received another year. After that year they were able to adopt the child. They had a little trouble in Italy getting a visa, but they were able to get the details worked out and the child now lives with the family in Italy.

I was interested in knowing more about that process. We were hoping to meet with her lawyer the following week.

We went to another orphanage in downtown Mombasa called Baby Life Rescue. We were shocked to realize that the person who runs it was Peter Mutua whom I had met when we had our initial parent meeting to start the ideas flowing for PARC a few years ago. We had also seen him earlier that day at the PARC kickoff event. He and his wife, Selpher, previously ran the only baby orphanage in Mombasa – New Life, which was located downtown.

New Life wanted to sell their most expensive property for some other ventures, and since this location was downtown, they sold that property. Then New Life offered Peter and his wife the option of starting their new center somewhere else. But they chose to stay in Mombasa and start up their own baby orphanage. He believes that God will provide funds every day, as he has no specific sponsorships in place, and formula alone costs the equivalent of US$15 per day for babies. He hopes to be able to start running a day care center to provide funds for the orphanage. (How ironic is it that Sue and I run day care facilities?) He has since done some market research, and developed and distributed his business plan, and the idea looks viable. Now, they needed the start-up funds.

Peter and Selpher have been doing a fabulous job. They already had a few kids and lots of space inside for babies. But they were not getting as many placements as they would like because the corruption within hospitals has been a major problem. Their facility doesn't have a lot of outside space for children to play, and they are in a downtown area which can be problematic. But their facility can hold a lot more babies than they currently have. In fact there are sufficient beds for a lot more children, although they don't have many toys or playthings for the children.

Sue and I began planning to host a Kenyan baby shower in conjunction with the Lutheran Woman's Missionary League at Hales Corners Lutheran Church in September of 2012. We were also going to organize a drive for formula, toys, boys' clothes, and baby equipment. Fox River was going to ship a cargo container to Kenya in the fall of 2012, and had given us some space in that container, for which we were very thankful. We had looked into shipping our own container and it would have cost US$5,500 for the smallest one that would fit into the back of a UPS truck. That cost was beyond our budget range. I could fly it there in person a few times for that cost. God has worked it all out.

Our next stop was Wana Wa Mola Boys Home. This is where Daniel, a Ugandan, and Mimi, his wife, from the Netherlands, take in boys from the street and teach them about God and how to live off the streets. They have tutors at the home for children who are too far behind to be in school. Some of them are in school

130

full time. It's a very nice home, where about 13 boys, aged five to 14 live.

While we were there, the boys were working very hard on school homework, and getting haircuts. They were hesitant, but glad to see us. We began with a tour. They were hoping to finish off a back space for a better tutoring room and hopefully an office for the home. At this time they just did the office work in the boys' dining room and living room. They really only needed a bathroom door and a little paint, and some hands to move some things, for example, better chairs for the boys. For tutoring, they have plastic high-top tables and stools without backs to sit on.

We started off with the younger boys, doing the craft project, using their fingerprints to make pictures. They were really good at drawing. The older boys wrote out a few sentences about themselves for us to take home. They are a very creative bunch and they had fun doing both the projects. It would be great to have a creative (music and art) man mentor these boys once in a while. We noted that they could also use some help on their website. They had one, but it was very basic and empty.

We had the boys gather around to listen to a Gospel story. They really seemed to enjoy the pictures especially. Sue read while I showed the kids the pictures. Then we talked about what the book meant. The older English-speaking kids seemed to understand. Then Paul talked to the younger ones in Swahili for a bit.

Daniel, the person who runs the home, was excited to have people from outside come in to teach the boys the similar messages they were trying to instill in them, as well as giving them something fun to do for a while. Daniel invited us 'across the street' to his other property for the older boys the next day.

Later, when we returned to the place where we were staying, we read through the cards that the boys had written, and we were both in tears. Some of their stories told how grateful they were for us to be there, and that was before we had done anything with them. Some had been on the street since the age of ten or before, and four years or more before they went to the home. They were well behaved and so grateful to God to be at the home. We were so impressed that we decided we had to go back for a quick visit before we had to leave, and we scrounged around to find them some treats to leave with them. Some of their stories are written in their own words in Chapter 8, *Remember Me*.

Wana Wa Mola II began in January 2012. It's a location for older boys who might not finish school as they are too old to go back and complete the grades. Instead they will do vocational training so they have a good chance to find employment.

We met the music teacher and the day-time Christian leader of the home. They showed us the place, which was small but nice. At that stage they desperately needed a well. Since everyone spoke and understood English quite well, we changed our approach.

We had a worship session where twin brothers, Francis and Peter (the only boys there during the day) sang and played guitar for us. We noted that they needed a new guitar. Their's was a cheap guitar that one can buy from Wal-Mart. It was difficult to play. But the boys obviously loved music. They said they wanted to be recording artists called TOB (Twins of Brothers). Hopefully, Paul can get them some good Christian music that they would like.

We took a page of the Gospel story and read it aloud, and then discussed it. We handed out name tags and talked about them and how much power we have with the Holy Spirit. Then we all shared things we were struggling with.

The boys indicated that they struggled with listening to rappers that were not positive for them. Daniel and Paul shared how they struggled with that, too, and how they replaced it with good Christian rap. The boys shared about how hard it was not to lie to try to get food or other things they needed, given their past life on the streets. We talked about the fact that, either you trusted

God or you trusted yourself. God has the power and we do not, and while it was difficult to trust God at first to cover your needs, once you do it a few times you will see how He comes through. Then it becomes easier and easier to trust Him in the future. How often do we all do this – like for a 'good' cause or reason, it's just a white lie?

I had shared how my biggest struggle was getting ahead of God. They wanted to know more details about that. Of course, I broke down crying as they asked me to tell my story about Kenya. It was embarrassing. Being sick and not sleeping enough had brought back my constant tears over Kenya the past few days. When I first started this journey, my pastor would always say he had to scope me out in the crowd before he started talking so he could make sure to avoid looking my way as I would be crying so hard, it was difficult for him to stay in control and finish his words.

Seeing pictures or hearing Kenyan voices would bring me to immediate tears. At this point, on that trip, everything I saw reduced me to tears – poverty, despair, and very little hope. It is all very hard to look at when you're not fully rested and fully connected to God. Add the stress of making a major decision about whether or not to purchase a piece of property does not make it any easier… and worrying that I was getting ahead of God on that score.

The Christian leader of the home asked how we could encourage the boys, from keeping up their dreams, to working hard. After hearing Rashid's story about not being able to complete high school, yet still moving onward with his life in great ways, we saw that it was a great chance for him to share his story of encouragement with the boys. Rashid was our driver, but he did so many other things for us. He would go far above and beyond every time, every day. He went to all our events with us, and helped any way he could, as bodyguard, banker, secretary, interpreter and fell into many other roles. Anyway, we all shared and then I was asked to close in prayer. We wished them the best of luck in all they did and advised them not to 'get ahead' of God.

Upeinde was the largest baby orphanage we found in Mombasa. And we didn't want to leave.

There were 13 babies in this orphanage, all laid out on blankets ready to 'play'. It is run by Patrick, an Australian, and Tammy, whom I think is Kenyan. They had just opened the orphanage in October 2011. It was small but sufficient for the number of babies they had. They were paying a lot for rent and milk formula. We discovered that they had a lot of clothes (mostly for girls), and not very much equipment. Since the babies spent so much time lying down, it was clear that they were in desperate need of bumbo chairs and exersaucers. They were way behind in sitting, although this was not to say they were not wonderfully cared for. They simply didn't have the resources we have for our kids. They take babies who need lots of medical support – tube feedings and so on. Tammy has been fighting the hospitals. She spends time in the hospitals with their babies, thus she sees a lot of what is going on there. The hospitals have been holding onto babies for four to five months and their weight decreases while they are there. They're waiting for the best bribe they can get from the Children's Department and/or a Children's Home for them to release the baby.

I was looking forward to working with Tammy and Vicky (the Kenyan lawyer) on getting this issue out in the open, and stopping this from happening, so the babies go where they need to be immediately. A lot of prayer over this is necessary, because right now, babies die during this process.

We had time for one more orphanage stop on this trip and we had saved the best for last.

Good Life Center in Mwtapa is an amazing place. This is how

I want all centers to look. The children live in separate houses; each house having up to 12 kids of various ages, with one mom and one aunt (only two babies per house, three toddlers, the rest are older). Each house is independent. They cook what they want, have chores for the kids and so on. They are a family unit and it feels like it when you walk in. It feels like foster care.

The next phase for them will be to build a 15-years-old-and-up building where teens can be more independent, getting ready to move out of the center to live on their own. Mercy, who is in charge and was so helpful, and George, their social worker, took us around on a long tour. They do work toward adoption there and I cannot wait to go back.

DESPERATION IS HARD TO SEE, BUT EVEN HARDER TO HEAR ABOUT

We went to Vipingo for a women's Bible study discussion about how all of us are ambassadors of Christ, not just the pastors. Pastor Paul had suggested the topic.

The women laughed when I said that many times women are the strong spiritual influence in people's lives. They are so undervalued. It's sad to see how unimportant they feel. It was a great lesson time, and then we formed a circle for prayer requests and to share our struggles. It was good to see how they all jumped right in. Sickness, parenting, and single-person issues comprised the most requests for prayer.

Nicole, a teacher at the Vipingo school, was an excellent interpreter. We handed out Swahili Bibles to almost everyone in attendance who did not already have a Bible... another way to share God's love and to see His work in action.

We also organized a Bible study group with the women of Bomani. We had the salvation message and then talked with them about how they can be 'ambassadors' for Christ. Most of the women were single parents, and we encouraged them to work together to support one other. They struggle with lack of food and poverty, and with parenting and how to deal with parenting issues. We encouraged them to teach the children the Bible and to use the Bible as their rule for their children. They also wanted to know how we discipline without 'caning' (using a cane to hit) the children. We taught them about time-outs. They wanted to know about what God says about being a single parent. They also asked a question concerning meeting someone who wants to marry a woman but does not want her children. Should they choose having children or the man? They are so desperate for basic needs that they are willing to give up their children to have their needs met. We left hoping to be able to get the women some Swahili Bibles, which cost about US$5.00 each.

It was really difficult to listen to their questions and answers. Talking about parenting, we were telling them to make sure the kids get good rest, and their response was that the kids don't sleep because they rock back and forth from hunger and cry all night because they are so hungry and don't have access to food. It was really hard to listen and not even have the slightest idea of what it means to live like they do.

It's humbling and makes me want to do more, even though I know I cannot solve these problems myself. Only God can solve them, but He needs us to help in His process. Sue and I are hoping to raise a little money to start up a small group for the single moms at the school so they can get some supplies to make jewelry and other crafts that they can then sell to church groups that come through the school. They will be cheap souvenirs for the groups and the women can probably live on that for a full year. I don't think this will take a large investment. Perhaps US$100 could give them a really, really good start. I'm hoping to get that money together from anyone who is willing to help.

Sue and I had some quiet time to talk and pray while relaxing in the pool for over an hour after our Bible study time. A lot of ideas came together for helping to facilitate women's Bible studies in Kenya. After discussions with the pastors of the church, Sue and I began encouraging Nicole and someone at Bomani to start their own weekly Bible study group with little things that we send via email, and anything they would like to speak about. I agreed to provide small verses and outlines for someone in Bomani, and Nicole in Vipingo, so they could lead the women in Bible study sometime during the week. The idea was that they would report prayer requests back to us and let us know when they needed more material.

Nicole responded immediately and was excited to continue the Bible study with the women. They had started the previous week and they had all enjoyed the message. In fact, a few of the women wrote to me on Facebook. Nicole was astonished. They had 25 people that week and expected to increase numbers the following week!

After some initial confusion, Emilly Akoth would be hosting the weekly Bible studies on Tuesday afternoons for the women at Bomani. They were doing just as well. They had around 20 people initially, and expected that number to grow week after week. It didn't take long for the women to get together to encourage one another... and they had a great time. God is awesome!

SOUTH COAST, HERE WE COME

Liz came with us on our trip to the South Coast. She had taken up Kristen's work in Kenya for Operation Give Hope, getting the biographies, stories, and pictures of the kids as well as keeping the website and Facebook account up-to-date for sponsors. She continued to work hard and share God's light with everyone.

Tribalism and Islam are very strong in the South Coast and that is one reason why it is very dark in that area. Though people claim to be Muslim, not many practice any formal religion there. There are very few mosques or other religious buildings. But I believe tribalism is more of a problem than the religious issue. Maybe that's why I like it so much, because it is easy to feel the darkness, and that makes me want to shine brighter for God than anywhere else. In the words of a native Kenyan:

"One of the biggest challenges on the coast is schooling. Because of the cultural and religious background of the coast, and capping it off with the tourist hotels and beaches along the coastline, most of the children in the region have been neglected in terms of schooling and technical skills.

"The culture has, most of all, neglected the girl child who is either married off at an early age or is introduced to child prostitution by parents or guardians. This equally applies to the boys who are introduced into gay life by the local beach boys and pimps.

"There are a number of primary schools in the area but very few secondary schools and colleges, and thus the need for such educational facilities to educate and give hope to the children of this region.

"(It is very interesting that along the coastline we have some of the world-class hotels and resorts that bring in a lot of money as revenue but most of the local people live in abject poverty and the essential social amenities are scarcely provided for). Thus, the idea of a secondary school is very timely and a welcomed blessing to the area - south Coast especially if you venture more into the interior.

"As a church, this is very important for us to find a way of the holistic ministry, that is, building the whole person."
Sylvester Opiyo, Central Diocese Projects

At Tiwi we first found my friend, Mwanarose. I didn't even know what room she was in, but God led me right to the room. It was the first one we walked into. She came along to help with the Standard 4 class as we did presentations. We read the kids' a Gospel story and then we talked to them about how they have God's power inside them with the Holy Spirit if they believe in Jesus; and how they need to use that power to figure out their purpose. They need to pray, read the Bible, and concentrate on how to hear from God… and then do what He tells them to do. Right now, that means studying and working very hard at school since they have a special privilege of being in school, and others in their community do not. It seemed very well received.

We had a good time talking with Vincent, Fred, and Issac about the fun day Ken and I had been planning for the summer trip. The business student girls from Alverno, as well as family and friends, and Facebook friends, have been collecting baseball hats for me. We wanted to be able to give a baseball hat to each of the kids and then teach a lesson about God protecting us, which is better than the hats. We needed at least 350 hats so were praying God would bring them in. They were all very excited about what we would be doing with the kids on the 'fun day'. In the summer, we were planning to do a career exploration day with the older kids. We hoped to be able take some Kenyan teachers, lawyers, doctors, and engineers with us to Tiwi to talk with the fifth to eighth graders so they could make an educated decision on what they might want to do when they grow up, and just have some fun playing with the kids and doing art projects with the lower grades.

Leaving Tiwi is always hard for me. As I was hugging Mwanarose goodbye, Sue got a great picture of her face. She had such a smile, it made the whole trip worth it just to see that precious face. I prayed that God would keep her safe and that she would stay in school until she graduates from law school like her surrogate mother! We'll see.

Then we were off to Tumaini. We did a quick visit to Mwangda, the school with a desperate water situation. Pastor Steven and his wife Monica greeted us. It was still heart-breaking there.

One year later, in November 2011, the good news was that we were able to install a well at the site of this school, which was a blessing. The other good news was that since August 2011, the children at this school had been receiving food daily through Manna Worldwide. That will keep more kids in the school.

There was still a lot of work needed. For instance, the buildings were still mud hut structures and they didn't have proper bathrooms, but there was some improvement... and hope.

I was planning to return to Kenya in June 2012 with someone from Risen Savior Lutheran Church in Franklin, Wisconsin. We hope that, after his visit, his church might consider sponsoring that school to give it the proper hope a church of God needs so we can see more change in the community.

PROPERTY? I'M NOT READY FOR THIS

Shortly after arriving on this particular trip, we met with Hellen and Vicky and they took us to view a property for a possible site of the offices of Pilgrim's Adoption Resource Center (PARC). There was a building that had been little more than half-built by a German man. The building had the bones of what we needed, a conference room and office on the first floor, and then lots of space upstairs to work with kids.

This possibility turned me into a tailspin. I was so scared, yet excited, and not sure what do to. I wanted to make sure this was God's plan. Even though everyone I have met in Kenya through God's plan, surely not my own, I wasn't sure. This was a great opportunity; we would be getting the building at the price of what the land alone was worth, which was a great start.

Could I do this? Was this possible? The purchase price would be somewhere around US$140,000 to US$150,000 plus contractor expenses to finish. We figured that we might be able to get a mortgage, but we would have to put 20 percent down for sure, plus most likely pay for the contractor fees outside of the mortgage. Though it was a good deal, it was a lot of money and I didn't know that was God's plan. But it seemed too good to pass on.

I had been praying all day and all I kept hearing was: "My strength is enough for you". I was not sure what that meant, but I would have to think it meant God would take care of this one way or the other, I must just do what He says.

I was reading the book, *The Shelter of God's Promises* by Shelia Walsh, when I got home, and the chapter I read was about grace and strength. It said God is glorified when, in our weakness, we lean on His strength. We bring all we have, and it is not enough, and it leaves us feeling tripped up, and sends us running into the night feeling abandoned and alone. But if we will listen for a moment, we will hear the music that pierces our shame and calls to the party all who are weak and find their strength in God alone. I had been relying on His strength physically since Tuesday the previous week, when I got really sick, so I know that feeling and now I guessed it was time to continue that trust.

Analyzing situations has been a real problem for me. Being trained as a lawyer, that's what I do. That's what people have paid me to do for years… to analyze everything and decide on the best possible approach. It's very hard for me **not** to sit down and write out pros and cons and then start researching the various options and looking into new options. That was exactly what I wanted to do. That was what I felt would bring peace and control to my mind, at least over this situation. Instead, I spent all our spare time praying for direction. Swimming and trying to relax, and not figure this out.

It was not easy at all. It was a constant struggle that took a toll on me emotionally and physically. Finally, on the Saturday morning, it became clear to me. I was running to the beach that morning, and looking out over the ocean, there was finally some peace for my struggling mind. If God could take care of keeping the oceans where they needed to be, He could take care of my small problems, even if they seemed large to me. To Him it is just another thing. The oceans are a much larger issue than whether or not to buy some piece of property and the financial issues that come with that. If God has the oceans under control and has since creation, He can handle a property decision.

That brought me a full and final peace without having to constantly remind myself to be peaceful. Even though I would like to run the other way right now, I will stand and let God use me to be His vessel in Kenya, even if it scares me out of my mind.

A few days later we went out to the property with Pastor Allan and he indicated it was in a very good area and available at a very good price. Alan said he felt the property alone would be worth over 8-million schillings (approximately US$98,000), and then to get a two-story facility on top of that for 13 schillings (approximately US$160,000) was a very good deal. Allan also thought the renovations would be approximately 3-million schillings (approximately US$37,000), which is what the contractor had told Vicky and Hellen on their description of the building. Unfortunately, once the owners saw all the cars and white people visiting the property, they raised the price. Welcome to Kenya. White skin clearly equals lots of money in their minds.

Later that same week, Vicky, Hellen and I went to look at another property in Mtwapa for a possible site for a resource center and orphanage. This property was large, but the building was nearly a shell for around the same price as the other, and without walls or a gate. God was taking care of it. He closed one door to open another. We were going to have to wait and see what happened.

The next day, we were at Ingili, another school and church run by Bobby and Lisa Bechtel, close to Mombasa. This was where Pastor Allan preached every week. He showed Sue around the school. Then, just as an aside, as we were talking in the dining hall, he said he was talking with a Christian friend of his about the adoption mission we were working on. This friend just happens to have some property rights off the road in Mtwapa that she was willing to sell significantly cheaper to help with the Christian mission. The property should sell for US$160,000 or more but she was willing to sell for US$48,000. That was another chilling God moment. We were to meet up later to view the property, even though it was only a vacant lot.

This was yet another example of letting God use His strength and not mine. What more was there to say?

AFTER YEARS OF WORK, THINGS ARE COMING TOGETHER!

A month or two before I left I forwarded some money to Hellen and Vicky, and they set up a public kick-off event in Kenya at a day care center for PARC (Pilgrims Adoption Resource Center). We had lawyers, doctors, and other professionals and adoptive families as well as potential adoptive families.

We also had the only adoption agency in Mombasa – Little Angels – represented by Grace there with us. At the event, we spoke about what PARC was, and will be, and who we were. We had some interactive games to get to know people and lighten the mood, and get people engaged. We also had a pastor speak on adoption. It was a sermon on why we should adopt and how God adopted us, which is an example to us.

We broke them into three smaller groups that discussed issues they saw that needed to be addressed. Each group had about 20 people in it and they each elected two group leaders so it would be easier to communicate in the future.

We also asked them to become members of the group to have some start up funds to do the work that we were working on.

They did an excellent job organizing the event. There were people of all faiths present at the event, which was good to see. This is a Christ-centered organization so it has become a great opportunity to reach out to non-Christians on a joint project. There was a large turnout. Being hosted at a pre-school, there was plenty of room for the kids to run around and have fun and we had an inflatable bouncy thing for the older kids. The cost of the event was about US$950, but it was definitely worth every penny for the turnout and the encouraging support from the professionals and parents.

The master of ceremonies was a teacher at SOS, at the Children's Department, and he did such a fantastic job wrapping up and pulling all the speakers together and keeping the focus on PARC's vision – a family for every child and a child for every family. He also highlighted their mission of being a *Christ-centered ministry that reaches out to all faiths and raises awareness and helps to support children without a parent, pregnant woman, and families without children.*

The parents had wonderful ideas on what to work on – some that we had heard before and some new ones. One man, Abdul, suggested we have an international adoption day every year and get embassies maybe to participate with it to promote it. We could start with some smaller ones around here in Mombasa and take it to Nairobi (where the embassies are) in a few years. That was an exciting idea and would be good to implement in November – International Adoption Month – which was probably why God was leading me to return to Kenya in November.

Nobody wanted to leave.

We started at 10 am and at 4 pm people were still there in full force and not showing any signs of leaving! But Vicky, Hellen and I had to go.

A few days later, Sue and I went downtown through horrible traffic, to meet with Grace from Little Angel's. This was the only adoption agency working in Mombasa at that stage, although they were not directly connected with any babies in Mombasa at that point. Little Angel's would probably be moving back to Nairobi soon as they could not warrant having the office in Mombasa because not enough adoptions were happening.

Grace gave suggestions on how to educate the police and hospitals and gave feedback on the adoption event. She also gave us a listing of the Children's Homes she had been working on developing relationships with, which gave me half of the places we were able to visit.

GOD'S FLIGHT DELAY

We waited in line at Kenya Airways for our 45-minute flight from Mombasa to Nairobi. After about 20 minutes, a lady waltzed out ever so slowly to tell us that we must have booked online as the flight we were there for didn't exist and that the 'real' flight was leaving at 9.40 am not 7.40 am. Another welcome to life in Kenya!

Though I was frustrated, as we got up early for this flight and had a whole day planned for Nairobi, I asked politely why they did not inform us of that as I had booked long ago and they had an email address and phone listed that was checked regularly. She never did answer me, but instead stamped us for the Safari Lounge where we got breakfast and free drinks. Sue got coffee for the first time during the trip, as well as WIFI, and most importantly, air conditioning! March had been very warm in Kenya (to put it mildly).

This had definitely been a God delay. Sue and I spent the time to review our notes of all our 'to dos' when we got home. It was at least four pages if not more, single spaced. Then we had a few extra minutes as they indicated the flight would be delayed by another 30 minutes; so we were brainstorming ideas on the orphanage. After very little discussion, 'New Heart Family – Kenya' came to life. It was perfect as the orphanage we were looking at would be for adoptions, but we also needed to have space for the children to grow, and in a foster family situation as well.

The orphanage we went to Good Life in Mtwapa had been perfect; a 'mom' and an 'aunt' with 12 kids, all different ages. The older ones helped clean, cook and look after the younger ones when necessary, and it feels totally like a family, not an institution.

And we wanted these kids, the staff, and the whole community surrounding it to have a New Heart with God. It was perfect. We had ideas for the logo and we wanted to sell T-shirts and some other things to raise money. We weren't sure how to go about doing that, but that was one of things on the new 'to-do' list.

We also came up with the idea of Tumaini Tuesdays (meaning hope in Swahili). To pray for the nation of Kenya, the missionaries, the schools, the communities, and also for direction on what to do, how to do it, and also to take some of the 'to-dos' and start working on them together. Really keeping each other accountable to what God was calling us to do.

God was really at work on this flight delay.

Firstly, we got many of our ideas together.

Secondly, it had stormed and rained really hard in Nairobi all morning anyway, so we wouldn't have gotten much accomplished anyway.

God is working, all the time, even during flight delays.

MAKING THE MOST OF TRAFFIC
FUND RAISING GOD'S WAY

Traffic was bad, and with all the driving, being stuck in traffic for hours and hours at a time, we made the most of it. We were making lists of US companies that were advertising and selling in Kenya, so we could ask them for donations in the future.

As I have already shared, it is difficult to get money for international missions, but if these companies are making money on the international people, then they can help with international missions. Johnson and Johnson, Shell, Hershey, Cadbury, FedEx, Kenya Airways/Delta, Avis, Subaru, Audi, Toyota, Citibank, Samsung, LG, Black and Decker, Kentucky Fried Chicken, Barclays, Nestle, Goodyear, Dunlap Tires, CAT – caterpillar Mantroc, and Coca-Cola; all of them do heavy advertising and sales in Kenya. I would love to have personal contacts at all these places.

So we have had all these ideas on fund raising and I've been through this deal before. Spending hours on organizing fund raisers that bring in nothing or less than the funds it has cost to put on the event. So I was praying about how God would have me fund-raise specifically for this US$48,000 piece of property.

At this point I was awakened in the middle of the night, probably the only time God can find me with my mouth shut and ready to listen! And I got the message, "Sell crafts". Are you kidding me? We were talking about US$48,000 here, not US$500. Crafts are not the most cost-effective way to go about this type of venture, God. And then I remembered that this was God's project and that I've tried things my way before, and they ended up losing money.

As I prayed on it further, God led me to Eve. Remember Eve, the woman doing the jewelry-making business with women at her church, who will soon be starting the same business at Bomani, and looking for a place to sell in the States? That's right.

So we stopped and picked up almost all of the jewelry that Eve had. Then God led me to the shop where we get so many beautiful bags from. The Shanzu Girl Guides run a shop that brings in disabled women and gives them housing, and trains them on how to use a sewing machine and then make various items – bathroom bags, purses, beach bags, lap top bags, and clothing – for two years, and then gives them a sewing machine so they can make a living outside of the property. The bags are fantastic; it's one of the stores that you visit knowing that you don't need anything. But the colors are so mesmerizing that you cannot help but buy five or six items. It's such a worthy cause. So we stopped there and bought a few things to sell back home to raise money.

We bought all these things on faith that God would work it out and find a place to sell them. Through God's leading, we have been at the South Milwaukee's farmers' market a few times making sales and donations every time. We also, after hours of work, modeling, and thought from myself and my intern, Elyse Kohlbeck who has done marvelous work, were able to get a website uploaded – africanbags.intuitwebsites.com – where the purses and bags are available for purchase to help two great causes at one time. We are still working on figuring out how to handle the African jewelry that we have a lot of for sale, but God has been faithful so far and I know He will continue to be, if I will just listen and do what He says.

KIBERIA - REALITY

Kibera is the largest slum in Africa and one of the largest in the world. Sixty percent of Nairobi's population lives in Kibera and it is one square mile. More than 1.5-million people live within that mile. Small tin roof and side shacks comprise the housing.

Garbage and human refuse line the streets. It was very muddy as it has been very rainy there for the past few days, but you don't know if the mud is from the rain or something else. There is no adequate sanitation and sewage is not disposed of properly, so there is always 'waste' in the streets.

Lots of street 'stores' line the streets as well. People are out in front of their tin houses selling whatever they make – tomatoes, maybe some dish they cooked up, or they have a sign for hair or nails, or whatever it may be.

The children there are in desperate need.

Due to sexual assaults and other reasons, more than 50 percent of the women are pregnant at any one time. Abortions are common, though illegal. Some statistics state that there are 100,000 children living there, and most are orphans due to HIV/AIDS. Walking around, all the kids yell, "Hello, how are you?" like it is a song or something. But most of them don't even know what they are saying. You hear it everywhere. They are lovely and loving children, living in a harsh, hard reality.

It's hard to do it justice in words – check out YouTube to watch a video of the place.

There are a lot of amazing works going on here. It is a very touchy place. It has a lot of needs, but people are coming in and not meeting them in the right ways necessarily. I am just finishing a book by Brian Fikkert and Steve Corbett, *When Helping Hurts: How to Alleviate Poverty Without Hurting the Poor... And Yourself* which discusses humanitarian efforts and how they can actually hurt more than help if they are not done in the correct way. It is an eye-opening book and it was funny to realize that most of the lessons they speak of in that book, God brought me through before starting any work here in Kenya.

Kibera is filled with people trying to help, which is good, but more of the right help is most needed. While we were walking, I met some wonderful people here on our journey. You can learn more about them in Chapter 8, *Remember Me.*

WE ARE ALL THE SAME INSIDE

On the way home, I was watching a movie about a black man receiving a white man's kidney by organ donation. The black man's kids asked the mom how their black dad could receive a white man's organs. She laughed a little with a glance toward the white man's father who was also in the waiting room, and said "We are all the same inside."

That really hit me. But I am definitely a minority in Kenya. It gives me another view of life. The point of life is to join together in as many ways as we can to help build each other up, not focus on our differences and tear each other down. I hope to be able to continue that, both in the United States and in Kenya, and I also hope to bring as many people as possible along for the journey. I think this brings to the forefront the issue of whether we are called to help in international missions or only domestic missions. If we are all the same inside, I think we are all called to work with and for everyone.

This trip was the bringing together of a lot of years of work half way around the world; developing so many more relationships, and identifying needs that can be easily filled. I cannot wait to see what God has in store next.

COMING HOME, CLARITY AND FOCUS

Writing this book has brought further clarity to my work in Kenya. There are many needs and it is so difficult to stay focused because a lot of the needs are easily met with a small amount of funds.

But looking back at all the situations God has placed before me, as well as situations in my life prior to Kenya, God has brought clarity to my purpose.

At the point of writing, my goal with Operation Give Hope – Adoption/Orphans was US$48,000 by November 1, 2012, to purchase a plot of land to build an Adoption Resource Center in which we can host education events and pregnancy crisis center. We also plan to rent it out for Christian events and for studies on evenings and weekends, to help keep our overhead down. Making a one-time donation or a monthly donation (anything) is appreciated.

We are able to support children for a lower dollar amount than most other organization out there because we don't have the high overhead of getting our name out there. Supporting a child in one of our schools for US$25/month through "operationgivehope. org" or "Operation Give Hope" – child sponsorship is a great way to make a difference. You can share this with your children or grandchildren. You can see their grades, their photos, a little about their favorites and the way they live. They very, very much appreciate it and send their thanks and they pray for their sponsors daily. Know that you are appreciated, loved, and prayed for often.

Thanks to all who support, and if you don't support yet, I would greatly encourage you to become a part of changing the world with only US$25 per month. It's an amazing feeling. I wish you could all be here to feel the energy of God working at these schools, it is indescribable, it is God.

There's really no more to say then – come join God at work.

This journey with Kenya and back again is less about coming from lawyer to missionary, and more about coming from "I can handle this life on my own" if I just try hard enough to...

"I cannot do anything without God's help".

I might work hard enough, and push things through, and get things to happen, and a few good things might even happen... but the amount of work and stress will far outweigh the benefit being received, and this work will not last because of that. Only God can bring these things to pass. Only God's power can change the world.

I know at the beginning of this journey, I did not believe that at all, I have only come to believe it by seeing it happen.

Thank you so much for joining me on this journey.

I hope you'll continue with me on this journey, both at my blog and in my next book.

8

REMEMBER ME

One of the reoccurring asks of the Kenyans is to be remembered. They feel like a forgotten people... forgotten by their own government and the world.

This chapter pays tribute to just a few of these magnificent people, in no particular order.

FRIENDS, FRIENDS, AND MORE FRIENDS

RASHID

One day, during dinner, we had the opportunity to hear Rashid's story. Rashid has been the driver for Fox River Christian Church in Kenya since 2008, the first year I visited, so I already knew a little about him, but it was good to hear his story in its entirety, and in more detail.

Rashid grew up in a village near Mombasa. His dad passed away when he was very, very young; not even a year old. His mom remarried a few years later and had more children. He went on to school, and an uncle paid for his high school education for two years. Then his mom fell sick and he missed a lot of school because he had to take care of her. It came to the point that he had to decide to either commit to school, or take care of his mom. He decided to drop out of school and take care of his mother, which he did until she was well again.

At the time he had an opportunity to get his drivers license. He began driving a small car and then worked his way up to bigger and bigger vehicles. Now he not only drives, but helps to organize and run a fleet of vehicles.

His wife, Lucy, has a small cooking business that she manages and runs. They have three boys, twins in high school and Dixon who is in the 6th grade.

We are so grateful to have him because he is much more than a driver.

PAUL

Over lunch at Yul's, a small restaurant and ice cream bar on the beach, we received a small snapshot of Paul's story.

He grew up around Nairobi in a non-Christian home. He accepted Christ at the age of 16, after seeing a dramatic presentation and talking with someone afterwards.

Paul doesn't like to talk about his himself. He would rather tell stories about the lives of the kids of Kenya. He is the head teacher and teen pastor at Vipingo, Crossroads Church, and does many things for Fox River's schools and the people who come to visit. He's also a marvelous travel agent!

Paul does great work for the people of Vipingo – teens and kids especially. Thanks, Paul!

PENNINAH

Penninah grew up in western Kenya. She had a single mother and two brothers. Together they struggled to make ends meet.

The Catholic Church paid some of her school fees, and her brother brought some money back to the family, but that only lasted a very short time. Her mom worked hard, selling whatever she could to raise money for rent and school fees.

Penninah was continually in and out of school because fees were not always there on time. She spent a year or more as a housekeeper and nanny for an extended family who promised to help pay her school fees but never did. She suffered much abuse in that situation. She didn't do well in her tests because she couldn't attend classes regularly. As a result, she had to repeat her senior year in order to get higher marks, but still had trouble getting into college.

Penninah and her mom spent their last bit of money to travel from western Kenya to Mombasa, to Shanzu Teacher College, realizing that she wasn't fully qualified, nor had the money for school. However, by the grace of God, she was admitted and they were able to work out the fee expense.

Penninah is now a teacher at the prestigious Light Academy in Nyali, Kenya, and is doing very well. She has returned to school for business studies and is currently both working and attending classes. She works hard all day and long into the night. She is grateful for her experiences because they made her who she is today, and she is now able to help others learn the same lessons. She is grateful, even though life has been tough for her. It's a formidable lesson to the rest of us. Penninah is a woman who has been through much trial and turmoil but still loves God. It shows.

LIZ

Liz grew up in Nairobi. Her family was not supportive of education, and wanted her to marry rather than go to high school. She had to run away to avoid marriage.

Liz got through high school in a rather unique way. She sat outside a minister's house every day. Finally they agreed to pay her school fees as a reward for her persistence. She also raised her seven or eight brothers and sisters and paid their school fees.

She works three jobs all day and long into the night. She also works with Operation Give Hope and is doing an outstanding job. I would love to have her persistence in my efforts for Kenya. Her bosses are lucky to have her. Hers is an exemplary sample of perseverance, dedication, and resilience. Liz is excellent on the computer. She also is thankful for all of her circumstances and is such an example of God's love to everyone she touches.

Visitors Through Liz's Eyes
"Enthusiasm and smiles on missionaries' faces is always there despite traffic, lost baggage, extremely hot weather, fatigue, bus breakdowns, or language barriers. This gives me hope. It is always humbling to see the missionaries walking into the villagers' houses. The schools and villagers of Bomani, Vipingo, Perani, Tiwi, and Tumaini know for sure that they have brothers and sisters miles away who truly love and care for them. They always await the arrival of the next group. I enjoy listening to the group talk to the missionaries while on the trip, talking about coming back and praying for funds and asking God to direct them on how they can help, or groaning about not wanting to go on safari, but rather spending another day with the children. It always shows where their heart and love is.

"Watching missionaries helps me to know that I do not have to feel so hopeless about what I see, but rather do what I can with what I have and, most importantly, to pray. I have become so attuned to what is going on and always excited for God to use me. Please come to visit, we would love to have you."
Elizabeth Kinuthia

ALLAN & EVE

I don't even know where to begin with Pastor Allan and his wife, Eve. They are the most God-loving, hard-working people I have ever met, which is no exaggeration. They work tirelessly day and night to make Kenya a better place for children.

Pastor Allan and Eve have two daughters of their own. They run a high school and a primary school and help to manage a secondary primary school as well as a church. That is only their charity work. Allan also networks for us and just follows God's lead on everything he does. Without Allan I would not have gotten anywhere in my work within Kenya because all my contacts have come from him.

This couple works continuously, raising funds, doing business, and brainstorming on better ways to serve the kids of Kenya. Allan and Eve also run several businesses including jewelry making, car rentals among many others. They have such a keen business sense that has been extremely helpful in all our efforts within Kenya. Eve supplies jewelry for my fund raising efforts, which also helps support the women at their church who make the jewelry.

I don't even know what else I can say about these two except that I can guarantee God is looking down on them and saying, "Well done good and faithful servants."

It is a blessing to be able to steal moments with them from their busy schedules while I'm there. Thank you so much, Allan and Eve, for all you do.

GEORGE OMONDI

George helps missionaries, Jim and Susie Horne, accomplish so much more in their ministry. He has helped us, too, and made us feel at home while on the trips when we stay with the Hornes.

George likes to stay in the background, so I don't have a lot of his story to tell. But he is truly wonderful, and has a strong gift of hospitality. For example, he ran into the house at 5.50 am, much to our surprise, to ask us to sign the guest book before we left on the last day. That's only one example of his dedication. He usually works in secret, but now, in this book, the whole world can see. We love you, George!

JOY

Joy has a wonderfully quiet disposition, yet she always demonstrates God's love. Joy owns a small business making fingernails and toenails look pretty, giving massages, and performing other salon services. If you are ever in Mombasa, make sure to look her up at Crossroads Church in Nyali.

At one point, she worked in a salon in Mombasa at the Milili Hotel and her friend Liz helped her. They worked well together. Sadly, a few years later, Liz passed away from pneumonia, even though she had been young and healthy. It just shows how different their culture is from ours. Though a doctor visit costs US$10-20 at most, Kenyans can't always afford it and there is no consistently free access to health care anywhere. Therefore, people generally don't even think of visiting a doctor. As a result, Joy has lost many people close to her in the last few years. Most of her family has passed.

Though lonely at times, Joy keeps moving forward with God. She has a great church family at Crossroads and I am so excited we are now working together on adoption work in Kenya.

MAUREEN

In April 2012, we got to meet Paul's cousin, Maureen. She walked with us around Kibera, which is the worst slum in Africa. There is something wrong with her leg and the doctors are not quite sure what it is, but she walks using a crutch, and finds it very painful. She needs to have surgery in Italy and they are working to raise money so she can get this done.

Maureen is attending a school for website design. She wishes to develop an address directory for Kibera. I have never seen a Yellow Pages-type publication in Kenya, even for businesses, much less for people. To find orphanages, I had to have our guide and friend, Paul search for them, and then ask if we could go and get contact information. Maureen's idea is a good one.

For the most part, my friend, Sue Huerta, walked with Maureen during the trip through some of the area. From Maureen, we got to know more details of life in Kibera. One of the most horrific and disturbing stories was that girls who are seven or eight months pregnant go to the local chemist to have abortions. By that time, the baby is still alive and is dumped in a pile in back of the store.

Women also drink bleach or other chemicals because they think it will kill the baby, but instead, it either kills them and/ or they get very sick and they still have their babies. It is difficult to hear this and do nothing about it. I guess that's the biggest challenge of working in a Third-World country. There is so much that needs to be done. To avoid further suffering, everything seems to be urgent, but, if one gets involved in everything, nothing will get accomplished. Though I wish I could get involved with these tragedies, I cannot do it all. If I even try to help there, nothing will get accomplished anywhere. It's still hard to hear and then walk away. Hopefully, in the near future, we will be able to educate these girls in Kibera about adoption, too. Then perhaps these situations will change.

We are thankful to Maureen for sharing the struggles of daily life in Kibera with us on a very real level and pray for her health to return quickly.

BENTA

While visiting Kibera in April 2012, we also met Benta, a woman who is working to get pregnant HIV positive women to doctors and on medicine, and to get medicine to their children right after they are born so they will possibly not be HIV positive in the future.

There is a chance to reverse the HIV diagnosis in a child if the mom doesn't breastfeed, provided she takes medicine while she is pregnant, and the infant gets medicine immediately and consistently. Benta is HIV positive herself but her children are not, although they were at birth. She had gotten them the medicine and it worked for them.

She also runs a small one-roomed school for HIV positive children. When we first went to the tin hut where she teaches, the kids were singing. We had just gone to say hello. We began to sing and play with the kids and then Benta told us that they were all HIV positive. The kids were very happy and looked healthy. I specifically remember Hiliary Clinton (a boy). I was holding him when Benta shared that they all had HIV and my heart broke. These kids were one year old up to maybe five, and they were all very sick. They will never have a day in their lives when they won't be sick. Not only that, but their parents are sick too, if their parents are even alive anymore. The kids sang for us and we all danced but my heart was heavy. I cried as we left. I hope to help Benta with her efforts when we start to raise money for our adoption center. I will tithe ten percent for her effort to buy medicine for the children and expectant moms.

Benta is one amazing woman. You can check them out on Facebook at Julie Hope Children and Rescue Centre.

Benta's Words

"We love friends. Carrie has been a nice friend who has consistently supported us by buying our curios (jewelry, purses, bead-work). I have psycho-support for mothers living HIV positive. We encourage them on prevention from mother-to-child transmission and most kids have turned HIV negative. We refer clients for treatment. I have started schooling at my day care, where we also do a feeding program for both the mothers and the kids. The women are supporting themselves and the children's day care center is supported through the purchase of these curios. Thanks."
Benta

STONE

We got to know Stone, who was also Paul's friend. He was a very young orphan in Nairobi. They moved him and some of his siblings (sisters) to the Salvation Army Children's Home in Mombasa. He was grateful to them for his faith in God. Then, when he had to leave, he at least had an example of how to let Jesus run his life.

Stone was an excellent swimmer and was able to get through high school with the government paying his fees because of his swimming ability. Then he began studying computer repair in college and earned a certificate; but he needs more schooling. He has applied more than 60 times to the government to get into college and they have denied him every time. When I last saw him he was trying to get a laptop and enroll in Collins University online to finish a business management degree.

I pray that Stone can find employment and/or schooling. Though he never said it, I felt like there was a real struggle going on for him.

STORIES FROM THE SCHOOLS
A COMMUNITY CHANGING

HALIMA'S STORY

Halima is the mother of two kids attending the school at Vipingo. After seeing what a difference the school and church had made in the Vipingo community, where she lives, she began a similar school for HIV-positive children next to the property. She used our school as a guide and they worked together.

Another astonishing story of life changing in Vipingo concerns a school that is sponsored by someone, or some organization in the United Kingdom. We spent a day at that school conducting a Super-Saturday activity fun day that included a Bible lesson, a craft, and some outdoor fun activities. God continues to work.

Sadly, Halima's children have since left our school though I believe they are still in school somewhere. We pray for her and her children to prosper.

Halima's Message

"Most of the parents of the children that are going to Crossroads [church] weren't attending any church. This means they didn't know much about God. So we have very many funny, funny [odd] crises in our villages. But now it's like everybody who's got a child in Crossroads is attracted to Crossroads; they are going to Crossroads. When they go to Crossroads as a church, they get all that is good according to God. Now everybody knows God in Vipingo because they are going to church. And I believe if somebody knows God and the whole community knows God and we live the way God wants. I believe we are going to be the best community in the future."
Halima, Crossroads Fellowship

TEACHER EMILLY, IN HER OWN WORDS

"God has done miracles at Bomani. Some parents could not afford to provide three meals in a day; they could only provide supper or go without meals. I thank Fox River for providing food for the kids. They eat at school and they are very healthy. Pupils are also growing spiritually as Pastor Bobby tells the Bible stories every week and they also attend Sunday services.

"In the community the people are blessed to have Neema Church at Bomani where they worship God. Many people are receiving JESUS. The Tuesday Bible study with the women is doing great and God is really using me to bring women to church. I must thank you for starting the Bible study at Bomani. I'm assuring you the number of women pushing into God will increase.

"Thank you, Carrie, for the work you are doing with us. We love you very much may GOD BLESS YOU ALL."
Emilly Akoth, teacher and Bible study leader

MWANAHMISI AND HER FAMILY, OPERATION GIVE HOPE

"Do you know the story of Mwanahamisi, who brought her mom to church?

"Mwanahamisi and her family have been Muslims all their lives. Coming to the school has helped her. She couldn't read or write though she had been going to madrasa (Islam studies). When we took her in at Crossroads Academy, Vipingo, things were very difficult for her and she struggled a lot. We had 'day camp' once when school was on hiatus. She came every day to the camp and she started showing an interest in Christianity and Bible stories. During that week, she gave her life to Christ and was baptized. After a few months, she brought her mom to church. Her mom also became a Christian.

"I believe that Mwanahamisi was a witness of Christ to her mom. That's only one of many similar stories."
Shared by Paul Odhiambo, head teacher at Crossroads Academy, Vipingo, Kenya

NELLY NYAVULLA DZIRO, HOPE FOUNDATION

"My name is Nelly Nyavulla Dziro. I'm a single mother of four kids. I was suffering with my kids before I knew Bomani church and New Life academy. New Life has sponsored my three kids namely Athumani, Vincent, and Lucky and is providing them with food, uniforms, and a Christian education. I am also thankful for Neema church because of the salvation I received and because I am spiritually uplifted. I am strong in the Lord and my life is changing day by day. Thank you for the work you are doing."
Shared by teacher, Emilly Akoth

SALIM KALU, HOPE FOUNDATION

"Salim Kalu is an orphan and is in KG 3 at New Life Academy. This school has done wonders in his life. He appreciates New Life for

providing education, food, and Bible teachings. Before New Life he would go without food since the relative he is staying with could not afford meals. He appreciates New Life because he is sure of getting breakfast and lunch. Imagine the life of Kalu without the Hope Foundation!"

Shared by Teacher, Emilly Akoth

ESTHER KARIS, OPERATION GIVE HOPE

"My name is Esther Karisa. I am 15 years old and in Class 5. At my age I should be in high school, but things have not been smooth sailing for me. For the past four years it was a challenge to attend school for I felt that at my age I should not be in school. The option was to go baby sitting at my relative's place. Last year I did so, helping her with the baby and house. I missed my classmates and teachers. I missed learning new stuff. I missed my family for I had run away from home.

"Eventually my teachers came over to talk with me and convince me that school, despite my age, was important. I am now back to school and working hard to achieve my dreams. I thank you all who prayed for me to come back. Teacher Daniel and Madam Rose counseled and guided me on this journey. I believe all this was/is possible because of the wonderful love of God. Just keep praying for me. Thank you all for your support."

Esther

"Esther is a lovely girl and one of the many who, at the age of 15, would be long-married and having babies. At her age, education is not considered important for her, hence the pressure. Please pray for her and girls with similar mindsets that God will help to overcome these ideas."

Shared by Liz Kinuthia of Operation Give Hope

MEBAKARI MATAO, OPERATION GIVE HOPE

"My name is Mebakari Matao. I'm 14 years old and in Standard 7 at Tiwi Baptist Academy. My aim of writing down this letter is to thank you for your endless support to our school. Personally, I must say that I would not be where I am today without the help you tirelessly offer this school. Not only have I benefited academically but also co-curricular activities like games, music just to mention but a few.

"I would like to assure you that I will not take this God-given chance to study in this prestigious school for granted. I will study hard and be focused always so as to succeed in my future plans. I pray that God gives you the strength to go on touching the hearts of the young boys and girls in our school. May you prosper in everything that you do.

Yours sincerely,"
Mebakari Matao

WANNA WA MOLA BOYS' LETTERS FROM MARCH 2012

*My name is **Elvis Mwaniurri**. I am 13 years old, and I am in Standard 6. My school is called Maweni Primary School. It is found in an area called Kisumu Ndogo. I'm working hard at school so I could be a surgery doctor. I really wish you all the best. Yours faithfully Elvis Mwanburi. Thank you for visiting us at WanaWa Mola Mission.*

*My name is **George**. In myself I am happy because God loves me and my friend. And I also want to thank Wana Wa Mola because they have take me to school. My school is called Maweni Primary and my class is three. I thank God because He protects me from the many accidents. Okay so I want to say God Bless me and you.*

My name is DIDA JIMMY. I am 16 years old. I come for Nairobi. I was street boy for four year and now I am in Wana Wa Mola home. I am in Class 6 in Makieni Primary School. My favorite game is footbul. I love to help street boys and I pray that He will help and protect us. I want to be a footbul player. I love my mother and father Ben. I like to read, so that my dreams will be good. Please pray for me in my exams and troubles. And I love you all and I love your work. Thanks for coming to our home.

My name is Mulei Joseph. I live in Wana Wa Mola. My school is Maweni Primary. I am in Class 1B. Thank God for you.

My name is John Juma. I like to draw. I am 12 years old. My school is Maweni. I love my friend. I like to play. Play with me. I like to Shera Sam. I love Wana Wa Mola because they serve and protect me. I thank God.

My name is Shadrack Krummel. I am 15 years old. I am Class 6 in Maweni Primary School. I Love God. God is my Saviour in my live. I come to Wana Wa Mola in 2009. I was happy to come at Wana wa Mola. I like drawing so much. When I grow up I will like to be missionary.

My name is Julius Kamau. I am a boy, but I don't have any brother or sister. I have been in the streets since 2007 until 2011 when Benon got me. I am in Class 8 and lucky enough, I am head prefect at school. I like music, and that is why I have written my own songs. I have forgotten everything about my past and I am looking forward to a successful future. Thank you so mush. I am proud to be who I am.

My name is Ali Kazungu. Wana Wa Mola is good home. We eat good food.

My name is James Mrombo. *I am 11 years old. I go to Maweni Primary School, Standard 4. I like school even my school is very good and to work hard. I love to play football. I like to read a story books and books.*

My name is Francis Kamau. *My home is Wana Wa Mola. You love to you we came here. Wana Wa Mola is good home. My name is school is Mawani Primary School. My class is 3B. I like play futball My church is Crossroads Nyali.*

My name is Hilda. *And I am the administrator at Wana Wa Mola home for street kids who undergo rehabilitation and their basic needs are cared for. The home consists of two houses. One is for the young kids and the other one is for older boys, that is, high school boys. The boys come from harsh backgrounds that consist of abusive families. Therefore, as you pray for us, pray for God's grace upon these boys and that the boys will find the free Gift of Salvation because it is only him who can heal and rehabilitate them.*

My name is Madam Florah Miwayo. *I am a teacher at Wana Wa Mola and I love God.*

FIND MORE IN THEIR OWN HANDWRITING

There are many other stories of life change in the children and staff at the schools. I invite you to go to operationgivehope.org and hopefoundation.co.ke to see some personally handwritten letters from the kids and staff about the life change occurring in Kenya. Here is a small sample of what you'll find there:

"I am nine years old. I am in standard two. My teachers name is Miss Nicole. Thank you for our desk and books we have. We learn many things. We are thank you because you have take care for us.

I am a Christian our church is called Crossroads Fellowship. We have learn many things from the Bible. The Bible is the book of God. The Bible teaches us to love one another and respect your parent. We are praying for you. God Bless you. Love One another."
Fancy Acheing, student

"I hope that you are doing fine. On my side, I am also well. My main aim for writing this is to tell you some of the benefits I received when I was learning there. I did my K.C.P.E. (examination) last year, and got 376 marks and I have been admitted to Kwale Boys High School, which is a good provincial school.

"I really thank everybody who has contributed to the success of this school. May God bless the work of their hands. I would also thank all my teachers who have never given up to ensure that I get quality education. I am one of those pupils who started learning here in KG1. It was difficult for us to be in school because of several problems, but we give glory to God for bringing us sponsors, like you, who has ensured pupils are learning in a comfortable environment. Personally, I confirmed from the K.C.P.E. results at the public schools that I could have beaten their index by ten points... I know that people from Tiwi society have gratitude to you because their children get education from qualified teachers... I also thanks Manna Worldwide feeding program, for sponsoring us with food... I have a dream of being a pilot."
Barran Musina, Tiwi Graduate

"Children and teachers are working hand in hand for the excel in academic level. High result in exams has led many parents from other schools to bring their children to our school."
Eunice Opunga, KG 1 Teacher, Tiwi Baptist Academy

"The entire school has greatly improved in academics, in general pupils from various class levels have really improved and most of

them can now score above average marks in exams. The school also performs very well in external exams, this includes, joint, zonal and district exams. In fact the school emerges top in the zone and district in most classes... The school has a very conducive environment for learning, this is enhanced by good, spacious and very clean classes. There are also different fields for various games..."
Alex Otsiolo, Staff, Tiwi Baptist Academy

"The moral well being of the school is so commendable; in fact the whole community has noticed and praised Tiwi Baptist Academy to be the most disciplined school around. This is enhanced through the constant guiding and counseling which is done in a loving manner."
Staff, Tiwi Baptist Academy

"Tiwi Baptist Academy is a Christian school whereby teachers and pupils are involved in a Christian way life. Pupils are taught on how to respect one another and love one another in the Lord."
Esther Rueben, Staff, Tiwi Baptist Academy

"It is not easy for the pupils to readily accept Jesus as they are mainly influence by their (Muslim) family. It is hoped that as they mature and gain independence from their families... when they proceed to High School they shall be able to make personal decisions. Nevertheless, there is a continued teaching of the Word of God and the Christians are growing in their faith."
Dorothy Kasivwa, teacher Tiwi Baptist Academy

"The school will grow into a very large education complex center and a health facility which will later transform the spiritual life of every member in the community.

"Tiwi Baptist Academy is a Christian school based on various fields to build up young minds and try to steer the pupils towards

greater achievements... In the future, I expect the pupils from Tiwi Baptist will change the entire community to be a better one. Through our hard work and support from the sponsors... we join our minds and efforts for their betterment."
Mr Alex Otsiolo, Staff, Tiwi Baptist Academy

"Great things are created a step at a time. I feel blessed to be a part of God's larger plan... a real cog in His workplace. When I return to Kenya this summer, I'll have a wider smile and an overflowing heart, knowing that, even in a tiny way, I may have helped just one of these kids, who deserve every break they can get."
Pat Molitor, visitor

"This experience really helped me to see that God was specifically working through me, to direct; through our parents to make sure their little ones were praying about and giving offering each Sunday, and through the kids who jumped up and down with excitement when we reached our goal. I feel like it really hit me that God uses me, and that I should listen up when He calls - because great things can happen!"
Nikki Boeck Nelson (had a fund raiser through Sunday school class)

9

MOVING FORWARD

WAYS OF MAKING A DIFFERENCE

RUNNING FOR GOD

Throughout this book I have mentioned a few ways God has shown me that I needed to work on my physical health while I'd been in Kenya... My clothes weren't fitting right; I wasn't physically able to do things others in the group had been doing (like climbing a mountain). Even looking at pictures from over the years I could see my weight was starting to get in the way of my work. So I began working out, walking, and step aerobics, all with zero results. I worked out three to four times a week for 30 minutes and I not only did not lose weight, in fact, I gained weight. I stepped up my workout schedule a month before my high school reunion, working out every day and really closely watching what I was eating still doing the type of working out and I got no results. This went on for a few years.

So when I sat down to do my New Year's resolutions in December 2011, which is far later than I normally liked to wait, this was top of my list of priorities.

The fact that this was later than I liked was one sign that I'm a control/organizing freak. But nonetheless, there I was, praying for the 'perfect' resolutions for me... in other words, the ones I would like to do, such as, travel to Hawaii, make a lot of money really easily, have perfect kids, read a good book. However, what came out of my hand and onto the screen was not that: "run a half marathon." Are you crazy? I hate running. I couldn't even run the mile in high school and now it was 20 years later than that, and nothing had improved to say the least. In fact it had deteriorated greatly. "God," I prayed, "I'll start to exercise more, I promise. I'll do the step workout, I'll walk more. I'll do whatever, but I don't run. Never have and never want to."

Yet, there is sits, in black and white: "run half a marathon."

After I got past negotiating and arguing with God, I sat with it. I prayed about it. I thought, "Okay, though I know I will never run a half marathon, what if I was to, what would I do? How would I break that goal down? I guess I would look into half marathons and find one to shoot for." There was no harm or even much effort in that. So I did that and found one scheduled for several months later.

Again, I thought that I would never run a half marathon, but what should I do next if I decided to do this? Start running, of course, even though I hate running and it was the middle of winter in Wisconsin. People don't run in the winter. "Run in the house then," said the thoughts in my head. "Start running for 30 minutes, four times a week in the house." This was crazy. People don't run in the house and that doesn't count. It's not really running if one can do it while watching Joyce Meyer, or while typing on the computer. Nevertheless, I ran, even though most people don't do it that way; it worked for me.

I was seeing results. I started running for longer periods of time, and then took it to the treadmill to run a 5K on. That I did not like, but then I took it outside and it was not too bad. I signed up for a few 5Ks.

I had blocked off a course that would work for me and I started with one lap, and then added another lap, and planned to add more and more laps until I reached 13.1 miles. The plan was laid, but plans and goals, though important and necessary, are not the key to success in any venture. The key is to stay focused on why I am running – for God, not me. It was not about weight loss or anything else (though that has been a nice side effect); that is not what it was for. It was for God. God told me to do it, so I don't have to like it, I just need to do it. The results will speak for themselves in joy, peace, and results – if I follow what God shows.

In fact running has had a lot of positive side-effects. While I'm running and wanting to stop because my side hurts or my this hurts or that hurts, God has taught me to keep running a little farther, and through that I have found that it doesn't hurt anymore after that, and I am able to keep going without pain.

God showed me that I can push my limits and be better for it, both physically and spiritually. I find that while I'm running, God talks to me. I learn so much more about Him and His strength and receive His encouragement. My time running brings clarity to things and brings me peace and comfort even if I'm not clear about things. When I'm out there and I feel like I just cannot go on. I put my head down towards the sidewalk or road in front of me and I hear God say, "You only have to make it one more step and I am here to push or reach for you at the next step. Just keep going". Somehow I am able to keep going. When I feel like I can never keep this up, God pulls me out of bed and reminds me, He is the one working through me, not me working for Him.

God led my husband to run with me; Though Chris at 6 foot 4 inches and I being 5 foot 5 inches, we didn't actually run together, we were out on the course at the same time and passed each other at times. He encourages me to keep running so he won't pass me twice, and I encourage him to get out of bed and get going in the morning. By doing this, not only am I learning more about God, but I'm also strengthening my marriage. This is something my husband wanted me to do with him years ago when he was training for a half marathon, and I told him, "I don't run." Now, look where God has brought me. Most importantly, it is following God's direction, not my own.

Though I still hate thinking about running, I find I don't mind any more. I might even say under my breath, very quietly, "I like to run." But don't tell anyone.

So the key to achieving any goals is two-fold.

One, know who you are doing it for, yourself or God.

Two, break down any goal into manageable parts. Only do the first part and focus on that, not the whole journey. Just this one part. I cannot think to myself that I will be running for the rest of my life. I break it down into parts and ask God what he wants me to do and do only that. I don't know what God will ask of me tomorrow; I can only hope that it will not be running, but if it is, I know just for today I will get through this run.

Like Eric Liddell in *Chariots of Fire* states to his sister while he is training for running in the Olympics, and she's concerned he's ignoring God's call for him to go to China as a missionary: "When I run, I feel God's pleasure." Though I would still say I hate the thought of running, I would also say, "When I run, I feel God's pleasure."

God's pleasure leads to revelation and wisdom. So why wouldn't you want to do what God has called you to do. It might not be running, but it could be going to Sudan, or adopting a child, or talking to a neighbor or co-worker about Christ. Whatever it is, go do it and let God show you His amazing power through you.

IF I CAN DO THIS, ANYONE CAN

Who am I? I am too busy and full of justifications and excuses. I have days where I'm barely keeping my head above water in many ways and wonder why I do what I do. I struggle with parenting my kids. I continue to make bad decisions of all kinds in all areas of my life. My point is, if I can do this, anyone can.

How do I do this? First, I admit who I am to myself and to God. Once we admit our faults and mistakes, God uses them to lead others. The admission is not to make us feel bad about what we have done; that's not the point. It is to help us realize that we don't need to do this alone. We can go it alone, and often I do, feeling stress, pressure, and as if I'm not good enough, but I don't have to do it that way.

Second, I can ask Someone to make up for those mistakes and come alongside me to help me. Jesus is the only one who can do that effectively. I can have Someone come alongside and help me, bring healing to those situations in my life I wish were never there, and then use those situations to help others, leaving the world a better place because of it.

That's what this book is about; demonstrating examples of areas in which I have had struggles. God is using these struggles to bring others through similar difficulties. I share my story as an example of what God can do through us, if we let Him. God can change people and situations. God can change communities. God can change the world. God can do these things with or without us; it is only us who miss out if we are unwilling. We need to be willing to do what He is asking us to do, knowing that it will produce amazing things if we let it.

You can make a difference. Are you ready to try?

IT'S RELATIONSHIP NOT RULES
PREFACE

I preface this section to let you know that I do not have the Bible memorized nor can I quote specific scripture verses. I'm not very good at that and I never liked it when people walked around spouting off memorized scripture at me. It felt like they had the

Bible memorized and I felt like I could never do that, so I might as well never try any of it.

Don't let the references give that impression. I simply used a computer program and typed in a word. The computer spit me out the verses that have helped me, so I thought I would share them. It was similar to my running journey with God… one scripture verse at a time; God always helps me when I need it, not the whole book at once.

As I look to the Bible for guidance in my life and why I do what I do, I reflect on James 1:27 in the New Living Translation (NLT): "Pure and genuine religion in the sight of God the Father means caring for orphans and widows in their distress and refusing to let the world corrupt you."

I love this verse because it brings me back to what I said at the start of this book. I am not a 'churchie' person. I never will be a 'churchie' person. I don't want to reflect or convey a particular religion or some set of rules people are to follow. That's not what life is about. This life is simply about one thing… relationship. That's all. Relationship with God. Relationship with others. Loving God and loving others. That's all there is. There ain't no more.

That makes it a littler simpler sometimes, for me at least. I don't judge anyone. I am in no position to judge anyone. I've done more than my share of misdeeds and continue to do so. Just yesterday I was yelling at my kids for no real reason except that I was upset about an email I had received. It comes back to whether or not I want to remain in that drama, fighting the world alone, or move out to something better, letting God handle it and just doing what He tells me to do. From my experience, 'something better' prevails every time, even if it is difficult and it doesn't make sense sometimes, like running. In the end, it's worth it and turns out so much better, as I choose to do the better part more and more, it gets easier and easier to do.

Don't let the world corrupt you into thinking that no matter what you do, it won't be enough. That's not true. Every little bit helps. A little goes along way with God.

There's a story in the Bible about an older woman, I think a widow, who went to the synagogue with less than a penny. She threw that in the plate as it went by. The guy next to her put a check in for US$1,000 thinking he was so much better than her for giving so much more. It goes on to say that the woman's offering of less than a penny is worth more than the US$1,000 because she gave all she had and the man could have given US$10,000, and it still would not have been a sacrifice for him. She gave her all.

The amount doesn't matter, be it in time or money. It's the act of doing it that God honors. He will multiply that one sacrificial penny to so much more. He cannot do as much with the US$1,000 gift that was given begrudgingly. My point in citing this story is to say, "Get out there and do the little part God is calling you to do. It can take only minutes; give your US$5, give your US$50,000. Whatever it is, do it."

Whatever sacrifice you make, God will honor it with so much more. Small acts make a big difference. God blesses our small acts to create bigger and bigger impact on the world. I struggled to understand that before. But now I have seen it firsthand and cannot deny it. My measly US$20 per month, that is 'wasted' away by me on a the drive-thru, a piece of clothing, a dinner out, changes and saves people's lives, both physically, through food, healthy water, and education, and spiritually. Only US$20; how can that be? I don't know, but I can tell you that it is.

The same thing is true with time. A little can go a very long way. I used to say I only have five minutes so I won't bother doing anything except maybe watch TV or something like that. Now instead, I use that to spend time with God looking for direction or doing something He has asked me to do. It doesn't take a lot of time, it just takes choosing that first. Before I turn on the TV or computer I need to do those things and then I am free to enjoy my

TV/computer or other time. So be purposeful in your money and your time and you can make a huge difference.

EXCUSES

Another verse that guides me is, 1 John 3:18 in the New Living Translation (NLT): "Dear children, let's not merely say that we love each other; let us show the truth by our actions."

This takes care of any and all excuses we might want to use. "My kids are too young", "I'm too old", "it's just not the right time", "I could never get off of work", "I don't have the money", "I'm so busy", and on and on.

We say we want to make a difference in the world or that we love God, but then we give any and all excuses we can think of to get out of doing it right now. "I'll do it, but not right now." That does no good. If not now, then when? We don't know how long we will be on this earth. There are perfect examples of that in this book. I'm sure Brooklyn and Josie wish they could take back their last day with their parent and say something different or do something more; but life is short, and we don't know when it will come to an end. Therefore, today is that day. We have to stop making excuses and start doing something little every day. Spend time before you watch TV or jump on the computer or while you're driving your kids around, and do something that God has been calling you to do. If you don't have anything yet, spend that time asking God what you should be doing. Quiet time, journaling, praying. Get up early; stay up late; do something with your kids, your husband, your grandkids, or with your friends.

Stop making excuses and get out there today.

FINDING YOUR DIFFERENCE

There are so many ways to make a difference and the key is praying and asking God for direction on where to start. He WILL direct your steps.

In 1 John 3:23 of the New Living Translation (NLT) John says: "And this is his commandment: We must believe in the name of his Son, Jesus Christ, and love one another, just as he commanded us." This verse brings me great comfort. It outlines our purpose. Believe in Jesus, means to TRUST GOD. Then, love one another. Don't judge or condemn people. Come alongside and love them. That's all. Wherever you are, believe in Jesus (trust in God) and love the people who are alongside you. That sums it up. It's easy enough, so do it.

Here are some good ideas on getting your mind ready to hear from God:

1. **Look back on your life and see what areas have been a pattern for you.** Look back at your childhood dreams and activities. What did you always want to be when you grew up? Is there something over your life that has been reoccurring over many, many years? For example, writing. In high school maybe you did a little writing. In work maybe you wrote letters or documents. Maybe you send a lot of thank you or encouragement notes. Maybe they were in totally different areas, but look through your life and see if you can find things to pull things together.

2. **What are some areas in your life that you are passionate about?** What activities do you live to do? What do you do that finds you losing total track of time as you are doing it? What things do you talk about all the time? What do you read about in books, online, in magazines, or in newspapers? If you had

179

a few hours free on a Saturday afternoon alone, what would you do? Ask your friends and family what they think you are passionate about.

3. **Spend a little time every day reading the Bible.** Even if you read one verse. If you don't know where to start, start with Proverbs, Psalms, or John. Try reading different versions of the Bible: NIV, Amplied, NLT, are a little easier to read than some others.

4. **Do the Bible Study – *Experiencing God* by Henry Blackaby.** This study will show you how to live a life for God, figuring out what that means and exactly how to do it. It's best if you can do it with a group, even if that means an online group. However, if you can't do it in a group, do it by yourself. I've done this study twice in two different groups. The second time I did the study, which was only a little over one year after I finished the first one, it felt like I was reading everything for the first time. So, even if you have done the study before, do it again!

5. **Read some books on finding your gifts and purpose.** These books should be spiritual books. Worldly purpose is temporary and won't lead to lasting purpose. It may give you momentary purpose at times, but you'll still be striving.

6. **Be concrete and direct in your giving and your experiences.** A great book *Radical: Taking Back Your Faith from the American Dream* by David Platt talks extensively about that and it has proven true in my life. God usually directs us in a focused way to make the most impact. Read this book to find out more details.

ACTION STEPS IN MAKING A DIFFERENCE

Now that you have spent some time finding areas that God might be leading you to, what next? Here are a few ideas that might get your mind rolling. The point is not **what** you do, just do something. Move forward and God will bring to you what you need.

1. **Share your stories of how God has changed your life with your family and friends.**

2. **Talk with your church.** Find the person in charge of missions or a Bible study group leader that can direct you. Find more information on what your church is doing locally and internationally.

3. **Look for needs that are not being met and bring them to your church.** That might be through finding an organization on Facebook or somewhere in your home town. Reach out to a smaller grass-roots organization – less overheard and more results and more personal. Find organizations on social media. Share their posts on Facebook or other social media so more people can see the work and when you are following blogs, click on the "follow me" button, it helps in many ways.

4. **Go to Kenya or anywhere with a missions group.** It is an unforgettable experience that will change your perspective and will show you needs.

5. **Spread the word about your favorite mission and the needs it has to family and friends.** Use simple conversation or have a dessert party with a speaker to share with them, or share your own pictures from a trip through Facebook or emailing.

6. **Once you have found a cause you wish to support, host an event to raise money.**

a) Organize quarterly recycling drives for cans at your church or in your neighborhood. Make an announcement that in three months, on a specific day, you will be recycling for your organization. Ask the congregation to bring their cans in after services on that weekend and then take them to the recycling place. Use the proceeds for a donation to support the work. This can be an ongoing event or a one-time event. This is free money. I love free (almost invented) money.

b) Organize a clothing drive or an equipment-type drive. For example, we did a Kenyan Baby Shower at Hales Corners Lutheran Church. The 'gently' used baby items were given to Peter and Selpher's Baby Life Rescue Center. We have also organized clothing drives through Facebook, asking for winter clothes and gloves for the homeless here in Milwaukee, and have taken the items to the Rescue Mission. It only takes a few minutes to put out a message, and a few minutes more to gather the items and deliver them.

c) Host a rummage sale for the cause. Collect items from family and friends. Post signs at the rummage that show where the profits are going. Hold your sale early in the rummage season – you will find it attracts more people. Hold it on the busiest road possible. Use online resources and Facebook to promote the rummage.

d) Contact the organization you find and see if they have anything you could do to help. For example, we at Operation Give Hope have sold purses, jewelry, and scarves made in Kenya. If people contact us, we can supply them with our products and help them host a party. Other organizations do similar things.

e) Penny drives with Sunday schools or classrooms where the winner gets a pizza.

There are endless ideas like this; brainstorm with your family and friends

6. **Donate time.**

a) Contact your organization to find out if they have any needs you might be able to help with. Maybe you're a good writer and they need someone to write a letter or a grant. Maybe you're good at website building and they need help with that. Maybe you're good at data entry and they need help with that. Perhaps it's graphic art. There are many other areas or ways in which organizations need help. Sometimes they just go without or they spend money to have their needs met.

b) Another idea – maybe you're a hairdresser. This might not be something an organization would need in their direct work, but we have had people at Fox River do a "Haircut-athon" to raise money for Kenya work. They advertised to the church for a few weeks, and then came to the church with their hair stylist friends and set up shop for a few hours on a Sunday. All donations were given to help the organization. Sometimes they also sold food and donated that money as well.

7. **Support by giving a direct financial contribution.**

a) Save coins. As the widow's mite (coin worth less than a penny) story cited earlier outlines, a little bit goes a long way. If you are purposeful about giving, God will bless that. Save your coins every day in a place that is public as a reminder to you and as an invitation to friends and family to contribute too. I keep mine in the kitchen, where I spend a lot of time. It's a constant reminder to keep focused.

b) Go without something small. Skip a hair cut and donate the money immediately. Don't plant flowers one year and donate that money to your organization. Cancel cable TV for a few months; donate the money immediately. The key is to not let that money sit in your checking account waiting to be used for another purpose. Take it out immediately and make a difference with it.

c) Check out your employer. A lot of employers offer matching money for donations. For example, if you donated $200 to an organization, they will match that and send the organization $200 as well. Some employers now even pay an organization per hour based on your volunteer hours. For example, you work for a food drive for eight hours; your company would then pay the food drive collection non-profit organization $6.00 per hour for the eight-hour shift; so they make $48.00 for the work that you did. What a win-win, time and money for the non-profit. US Bank, Northwestern Mutual, Quad-Graphics, GE Medical, and many other businesses have such wonderful programs. Check with your Human Resources Department about possible programs.

d) Choose a cause you are willing to make a sacrifice for. Go through your budget and decide how much you can donate monthly for a year. Contact your organization and tell them the amount, and when and how they can expect it. Ask them how these funds could be best used. After you make all the payments, follow up with the organization to see what a difference that made.

8. Any other way God may direct for your organization. Pray about it and ask God for guidance and direction.

Throughout this journey, God has led me to amazing places I would never have chosen for myself. I'm not a world traveler; I never wanted to travel much. The US is plenty big enough for my tastes. However, God has led me in another way. I'm so glad I listened and have been able to partner with Him and other wonderful people around the world and to bring people to Him.

I want to leave you with one last thought. Take a look through the picture section of this book on Pages 80 to 111.

If you look closely at the faces and the surroundings, you will see what Kenya looked like early on, and look at the eyes. You will also see slow changes. Though the pictures are not necessarily in date order, you can see it. Look at the surroundings. You can see the changes. You can see how the kids' faces are changing. The community is smiling and changing.

God is at work in Kenya and around the world. Will YOU join Him? I hope your answer is "yes".

ABOUT THE AUTHOR

Carrie Reichartz is a lawyer and small business owner in New Berlin, Wisconsin USA, where she was born and raised. She is wife to Chris and mom to her two children, Colton and Brooklyn, and step-mom to Lexie and Zach. She graduated from UW-Whitewater with a BS in psychology/criminal justice, and received her law degree from Marquette University Law School in Milwaukee, Wisconsin.

Carrie has always had a passion for working with and for children. She has worked as a guardian ad litem representing children's rights in court as a practicing lawyer for seven years. She has written for several legal publications and, shortly after being voted by her peers as a *Rising Stars* lawyer, she went to Kenya for the first time on a mission trip with Fox River Christian Church in 2008.

After her return from Kenya, Carrie closed her law office to open a home day care facility so she could be closer to her children and have more time to work on international issues. Currently she travels to Kenya two to three times per year and is working on developing a much needed pregnancy crisis/adoption education center near Mombasa.

She also raises funds for Christian schools and feeding centers in Kenya through Operation Give Hope. While in Kenya Carrie presents to girls at schools on focusing on their dreams and goals, rather than boys and relationships, showing how pregnancy would change those goals and how to avoid that. She also presents on various topics to churches, including what adoption is, as well as how God has worked in her life to bring her to this calling. Inspiring women to find hope and their own passion drives Carrie as she shares her struggles to encourage others.

Outside of working, she loves to read, scrapbook, and coach gymnastics.

FURTHER INFORMATION

Thank you so much for taking your time to experience Kenya with me. I hope you will continue this journey with God in Kenya.

WEBSITES:
kenyagivehope.com
To contact Carrie, book speaking engagements.
Love to hear how God has worked in your life.
www.operationgivehope.org
To learn more about projects going on in Kenya and to sponsor a child for US$25 per month.
www.hopefoundation.co.ke
To learn more about projects going on in Kenya and to sponsor a child for US$25 per month.

For more information about this book and to make sure you don't miss the release of my next book.

You can also Find Us and 'LIKE' on Facebook to receive up to date information.
www.facebook.com/pages/Operation-Give-Hope-OrphansAdoption
www.facebook.com/OperationGiveHope

I continue to write my blog at:
Kenyaadoptioncarrieandyou.blogspot.com
Become a follower.

SPONSORS

Finally, a very special thank to all the sponsors, without whom this book and this journey would never have been possible.

In particular, the following sponsors have made it possible for all the proceeds from this book to go directly to the children – we thank them so much for their help and support.

Little V.I.P. Preschool & Child Care
"Where Quality Comes Naturally From The Heart"
Wind Lake, WI 53185
262-895-2558
www.littlevipchildcare.com

Jennifer Torres
Marketing by JT
www.marketingbyjt.com
www.thepromocafe.com
marketingbyjt@aol.com
908-264-8111

Penny Swift
Editorial, design and book production services
pennyswift@vodamail.co.za
www.pennyswift.com

Made in the USA
Lexington, KY
22 February 2014